HIDDEN TREASURES

LIVERPOOL

Edited by Donna Samworth

First published in Great Britain in 2002 by
YOUNG WRITERS
Remus House,
Coltsfoot Drive,
Peterborough, PE2 9JX
Telephone (01733) 890066

HB ISBN 0 75433 982 3
SB ISBN 0 75433 983 1

FOREWORD

This year, the Young Writers' Hidden Treasures competition proudly presents a showcase of the best poetic talent from over 72,000 up-and-coming writers nationwide.

Young Writers was established in 1991 and we are still successful, even in today's technologically-led world, in promoting and encouraging the reading and writing of poetry.

The thought, effort, imagination and hard work put into each poem impressed us all, and once again, the task of selecting poems was a difficult one, but nevertheless, an enjoyable experience.

We hope you are as pleased as we are with the final selection and that you and your family continue to be entertained with *Hidden Treasures Liverpool* for many years to come.

CONTENTS

Aishea Evans	33
Alex Barry	33
Home 12	34
James Bigley	34
Terrylee Thomson	35
Michelle Lawson	35
Natasha Williams	36
Paul Fahey	36
Laura Ambrose	36
Home 12	37

Hunts Cross Primary School

Amy Holland-Rathmill	37
Sarah Harrison	38
Michelle Williams	39
Emma Taylor	39
Kelly Maguire	40
Kyle Buckley	40
Rebecca Fitzgerald	40
Robyn Hannah	41
Ricky McDonough	42
Peter Duffield	42
Ashley Purchase	43
Charlotte Fitzgerald	44
Alex Ashton	44
Aimee Evans	45
Michael Byrne	45
James McHugh	46
Michelle Kelly	46
Yolanda Hyland	47
Adam Saunders	47
Marvin Turner	48
Ross Balmforth	48
Katie Doran	49
Jennie Gervais	49
Rachel Bird	50
Peter Burke	50

Christopher Henshall	64
Adam Lonergan	65
Lyndsay Evans	65
Michael Wong	65
Joseph O'Neill	66
Darcy Slade	66
Amy Hawkens	66
Ryan Fitzpatrick	67
Melissa Mountaine	67
Jamie-Leigh Stockton	68
Lauren Corness	68
Megan Hopwood	69
Sean Owens	69
Louis Harpur	70
Megan Birchall	70
Charlotte Kelly	71
Katherine McLachlan	71
Richard Grierson	72
Katherine Clarke	72
Sophie Lamont	73
Stephen Farrell	73
Charlotte Hughes	74
Christopher McCormick	74

St Anthony Of Padua Primary School

Sarah-Jane Carr	75
Joseph Carroll	75
Kathryn Omar	76
Joseph Davis	76
Charlotte Kelly	77
Georgina Hoyle	78
Siobhan White	78
Adam Ward Thomas	79
Thomas Sewell	80
Kathryn Walby	80
Alexandra Mealand	81
Matthew Boyes	82

St Joseph's Primary School

Rachael O'Hare	82
Katie McLoughlin	83
Hayley Brennan	84

St Margaret Mary's Junior School

Kate Graham	84
Matthew Doyle	85
Philip Hynes	85
Sam Murphy	86
Jennifer Southern	86
Hannah Maher	87
Claire Cameron	88
Hannah Maloney	88
Anthony Silvano	89
Aaron Murphy	90
Robyn Mulvoy	90
Ann Power	91
Adam Dixon	92
Steffie Connell	92
Kayleigh Blackburn	93
Natalie Williams	94
Oliver Holmes	94
Michael Rowe	95
Laura Gregson	96
Robynn Hughes	96
Hollie Gregory	97
Stephanie Needham	98
Jade Clegg	98
Sara Walsh	98
Megan Austin	99
Josh Quinn	99
Robert Goudie	100
Hannah Ryan	100
Samuel Harris	101
Jack Ehlen	101
Andrew Lamkin	102
Catherine Kelly	102

The Poems

MY FRIEND ADAM

You are a pineapple, spiky and soft.
You are flames, hot and fast.
You are a BMW, smart and posh.
You are the colour red, hot and fast.
You are disco music, lively and fun.
You are a bed, comfy and snug.

Ross Cushion (7)
Blacklow Brow Primary School

MY WORLD IN COLOUR

You are an orange, shiny and fresh.
You are the sun, hot and burning.
You are a lime, shiny and cool.
You are the colour red and hard.
You are rap music, cool and rock.
You are a cushion, warm and lovely.

Ben Waldron (7)
Blacklow Brow Primary School

MY DAD

You are an orange, sweet and soft
You are sunshine, tight and fresh.
You are a BMW, soft and smart.
You are the colour blue, cool and calm.
You are disco music, lively and fun.
You are an armchair, small and soft.

Craig Mutch (8)
Blacklow Brow Primary School

MY MUM

You are a banana, soft and nice.
You are snow, cold and icy.
You are a Ferrari, cool and posh.
You are the colour lilac, nice and feathery.
You are party music, fun and great.
You are a black chair, snug and comfy.

Adam Duckworth (8)
Blacklow Brow Primary School

MY SISTER

You are a pineapple, hard and rough.
You are a storm, raging and crashing.
You are a Ferrari, revving its engine.
You are the colour red, with a fiery glow.
You are rock music, loud and mean.
You are a wooden bench, hard and crooked.

Liam Lannigan (8)
Blacklow Brow Primary School

MY DOG

You are a Ferrari, fast and clever.
You are gold, light and heavy.
You are lightning, strong and loud.
You are the colour red, a bull and smart.
You are a cushion, soft and comfy,
You are fire, hot and steamy.

Sean Givnan (7)
Blacklow Brow Primary School

MY COUSIN REBECCA

You are a strawberry, lovely and sweet.
You are light rain, gentle and smooth.
You are a limousine, squashy and comfy.
You are the colour red, hot and bright.
You are disco music, exciting and fun.
You are a cushion, fluffy and soft.

Jazmine Moody (8)
Blacklow Brow Primary School

EMMA BUNTON

You are a banana, blond and sweet.
You are like snow, nice and soft.
You are a Fiesta, comfy and gentle.
You are the colour yellow, bright and sweet.
You are disco music, fast and brilliant.
You are comfortable, warm and snug.

Liam Bell (7)
Blacklow Brow Primary School

MY MUM

You are a grape, sweet and smooth.
You are a rainbow, colourful and bright.
You are a blue bird, cuddly and soft.
You are the colour green, fresh and light.
You are some disco music, funky and fun.
You are a bed, snug and comfy.

Jennifer Bruce (8)
Blacklow Brow Primary School

THE AUTUMN TREASURES

The green emeralds with a sparkling hint,
Waiting patient for their time to surpass,
Rustling now amongst the summer breeze,
As the autumn treasures begin to bud.

The leaves turn shades of red, browns and oranges,
Drifting down towards the weather-beaten ground,
Ready to be hidden
Waiting until spring for their rebirth.

Autumn dawns on this radiant beauty,
As hammering rain beats the elderly leaves,
An intense red falls to the ground,
Separating quickly as exhaust fumes lick the road.

The leaves now bygone, the past, forgotten
Until spring recurred from the past
The trees now bare and stripped and crisp
Falling into the fingertips of the mist.

Of course those some still remaining,
Pondering over weather to live until life's limit,
Or to drop,
Like a forgotten teardrop welled up in an eyelid.

Antony Haddley (10)
Blacklow Brow Primary School

THE WITCH'S KITCHEN

Down in the witch's kitchen
I can see her stirring and sitting beside her is a black cat purring.
She looks in a cupboard to pick out mice
That she will use later on to make her spice.

Down in the witch's kitchen I can hear her cackle
Over the noise of her cauldron's crackle.

Down in the witch's kitchen there's a horrible smell
It's the bubbling ingredients of her wicked spell.

Helen Walsh (9)
Blacklow Brow Primary School

THE GIANT'S CASTLE

I walked into the giant's castle
I could see that there was a lot of hassle.
The giant has shouted at his wife
And hurt her with a knife.

Then I could hear the giant's feet
I thought I was going to be a small piece of meat.
He was coming closer and closer with a bang
He started to dance and he sang.

I went under a table and could smell something
It was the giant's food he was munching,
It was the smell of cheese
And the smell of peas.

As I walked across the castle floor
I felt it move so I hid behind a door,
Then something patted me
I turned around and it was a mouse called Lee.

The giant made soup
And I took a scoop
It tasted yuck
I think it was made of muck.

Hannah Thompson (8)
Blacklow Brow Primary School

THE EXPLORER'S ATTIC

The attic was dark
I could hear the dogs bark
But in this room
I stared in the gloom.
What I saw was a shock
There were piles of rock
And books and guns and maps
And lots of rucksacks.

The dust was so thick
It makes you feel sick
You could smell it and taste it
The draught even swirled it.
A volcano of dust
Was blown high in the sky
As I kicked a great pile
The smell was so vile.

I started to look at one odd looking book
The writing was old and the pictures were bold.
The writer had travelled thousands of miles
Through India, New Zealand,
Australia and England
Exploring and searching
For evidence of a king snake.
A snake with two heads
That fought with itself
So difficult to find
He went out of his mind
But he left notes, his maps and his coats.

As I sat and thought of this man
Who had fought
To see this rare snake
He spent all of his life
Exploring the world
For a glimpse of the snake.

Now his life's in this room
With spiders and gloom
The wind whistles and moans,
The beams creak and groan
The webs tickle your face,
Grit all over the place.
The dust makes you blind.
It's so sad when you think
This man wasted his life
Searching for this one snake.

What a mistake!

Scott Thompson (8)
Blacklow Brow Primary School

MY HIDDEN TREASURE

You are my guardian angel
You never let me down
You're with me every step of the way
When life's rolling round.

You love me unconditionally
Even when I've done wrong,
You are for me when I'm sick
And help me move along.

You're something money can never buy
From any shop or store
You are my greatest treasure.
Mum
I love you more and more.

Samantha Currie (9)
Blacklow Brow Primary School

TUCKED AWAY

I took the box into my hand
Dreaming into an imaginary land.
In this box was a wonderful place,
Gleaming into my wrinkling face.
This held everything dear to me,
Hidden away was the secret key.
It was waiting to be unfolded,
It may not be pretty, all dusty and moulded.
It held everything special to me,
All tucked away secretly.
All my memories from young to old,
All the stories that I've been told.
It slowly opened and all that was there,
Was an old rag and a lock of hair
It brought me back a lot of pleasure
Even though it wasn't much treasure.
I lifted it up once again,
And placed it on the windowpane.
To watch everyone go by,
To watch me when I laugh or cry.

Charlotte Benbow (10)
Blacklow Brow Primary School

THE EXPLORER'S ATTIC

Up the old, dusty stairs that creek on every step
To the door that leads to the explorer's attic
The old, rusty bolt that keeps the door closed,
The heavy door opens with a creek
As I feel for the light I feel silky cobwebs.
The light in the attic is dull from the dirt
A curled up whip, the adventures it might have had
In an old wooden chest lie tales of the past

8

An ugly mask and a very sharp spear from an African adventure
Ancient statues of Egyptian gods found inside a pharaoh's tomb.
In a pile in a corner are maps that show places of hidden treasure
West Indies, Africa, Egypt and China.
Others so strange I have never heard of
Closing the old, heavy door
Sliding back the rusty bolt
I leave the attic with my mind full of adventures.

Nathan Griffiths (9)
Blacklow Brow Primary School

MY SECRET TREASURE

At the bottom of the garden
In the winter's cold
I buried a secret treasure
That's better than any gold.

I go and see her every day
To see if she is fine
I'll always love her forever and ever
And she is mine.

If you don't know by now
I'll tell you what I found
It's something very special
Underneath the ground.

It's my cat Lucy
Buried forever and ever.
Under the rose bush
But I know she got a lot of pleasure.

Sophie Stockdale (10)
Blacklow Brow Primary School

TREASURES

T   rying hard to keep it a secret
R   eading the small microscopic writing
E   xited too much to keep it all mine
A   s I open the strange briefcase
S   o hard to keep it a secret
U   sing all my might to keep it all to myself
R   eading the small lettering again for the sake of it
E   xcitement from head to toe, from toe to head.
S   eeing nothing, but still a treasure.

Josh Birchall (11)
Blacklow Brow Primary School

THE MONSTER'S CAVE

The monster's cave is a dreadful place
It's cold and damp with not much space.
If you dare go alone
The walls are bare and made of stone.
Your voice it echoes around the cave,
Go in only if you feel very brave.

Jack Shaw (8)
Blacklow Brow Primary School

THE WITCH'S KITCHEN

In the witch's kitchen guess what I could see?
Purple daffodils, but what's for tea?

Lady finger, boys with girls made of toys
And chocolate potato Coys

In the witch's kitchen guess what I could see?
Bubbling, green potions and a frog floating in her tea.

In the witch's kitchen guess what I could see?
Butterfly wings and hog's knee!

Ruqayya Moynihan (8)
Blacklow Brow Primary School

FAMILY TREASURE

My coat over my shoulder, I ran to the garden
Yelling at my mum to let me go out.
The trees seem to get closer with every step
Spotted a case lying forgotten on the floor
I picked it up and put it on my knee
Starting to open it being careful and steady
Not a doubt at all
Put my hand inside and pulled a little glass photo of me and my family.

James Hibbert (10)
Blacklow Brow Primary School

LOST TREASURE

Deep in dark sea lays a gift for me
Dolphins protecting but protecting what? Nobody knows
Divers dive deep into the ocean searching, searching
Nothing is found, no sign of life, just a big stone.
Dust is everywhere, but I don't care not at all.
Down there I was trying to open it and then I did it!
Deep in the dark sea, lays a gift for me.

Sophie Gaffney (8)
Blacklow Brow Primary School

ANIMALS RULE

Chicks are so sweet they make a tune tweet, tweet.

Frogs are so dumb all they do is sit around like a plum.

In the world of a fly they get squashed and never say bye.

Never mind, my dog, he barks at the moon waiting for an alien
called Ragnarog.

Animals are the best, they're better than the rest.

Lee Givnan (10)
Blacklow Brow Primary School

MY LITTLE FRIEND

My little friend runs across the road
Here comes a car in fourth gear mode.
Honk, honk, beep, beep, the car makes some sounds,
But my friend just sits there on mounds and mounds . . .

My little, fluffy, feline friend
Makes it across the road but next time
Who knows?

Jonathan Keefe (9)
Blacklow Brow Primary School

SNOW

Enchanting, fascinating, it veers me spellbound
As I observe, it resides on the smooth ground.
It bids me welcome to its graceful glow,
Drifting majestically in a pure, pale bow.

The treasure brightens the cold wind and hail,
Weaving in-between each other's trails.
The stray final flake aimlessly descends,
The blizzard is over, the whiteness ends.

Gregg Gaffney (11)
Blacklow Brow Primary School

MY SPECIAL TREASURES
(In memory of my two grandads)

My two hidden treasures are
Up in the sky
I wish they did not have to die.
I miss them with all my heart
It shot at me like a sharp dart.
I know that they'll always be looking down at me
Until it's my turn to go up and join them.

Lauren Knowles (9)
Blacklow Brow Primary School

MY PET TREASURE

My tiny, white, ball of fluff
Is cute and cuddly
And loveable to play with.

She sleeps through the day
And wakes up to play
She is the best friend ever.

My bunny rabbit will always be my pet treasure.

Ashleigh Long (9) & Emma Gibson (10)
Blacklow Brow Primary School

HIDDEN TREASURE

I was under my bed
When I banged my head
Then I found a map
Along with a cap.
I wished I was under the sea,
That's where I wanted to be,
My wish came to me,
And I was under the sea.
Hunting for treasure,
Hoping for a lot of pleasure,
I saw a small chest,
In a shark's nest.
I got the treasure,
And it brought me a lot of pleasure.

Christopher Halliwell (10)
Blacklow Brow Primary School

THE WITCH'S KITCHEN

In the witch's kitchen
There are smells of all sorts
Witches' potions, simmering
In the dark, black, rusty, old cauldron.
The sound of witches' cackles
And bubbling potion brings shivers down my spine.
You would hate to see the witch that lives there
She has warts on her nose which also bring shivers
                              through my whole body.
It gives me goosebumps when I hear her witchy cackle!

Hannah Gibson (9)
Blacklow Brow Primary School

MY BROTHER KIERAN

Kieran is the best,
He is just like a cuddly bird in a nest,
Kieran is so soft and warm.

Kieran is so funny,
He's a little bunny,
Kieran likes to laugh, play and have fun,
He definitely loves his mum.

Kieran loves his dad the most,
Kieran only really likes custard, sweets, bottle and yoghurt,
Kieran is a baby boy
He is just like a toy.

Kieran loves anything on wheels,
But mostly he loves his bus.
He likes his sister to come and get him
And running around.

I like my brother.

Stephanie McVey (7)
Blacklow Brow Primary School

STORMY WEATHER

A storm is an outrageous bull,
A storm is a violent tornado,
A storm is a wild shark approaching its prey,
A storm is a gusty sandstorm,
So if you ever come across a storm
My advice is to run!

Robert Dean & Sam Robertson (10)
Blacklow Brow Primary School

MY HAMSTER SMUDGE

My hamster Smudge was a golden ball of energy,
Anything I could do, he could do better,
Running, jumping and climbing
He was a good hamster and a good friend.
When he was in his hamster ball he would always hit walls,
And he was always on the ball.

In my nan's back garden, he lies in a box and waits
For me to go and see him
Even though he's underground,
He is my hidden treasure and he always will be.

Smudge has died but he hasn't gone,
He will always be in my mind,
As life goes on.

Niall Blanchflower (10)
Blacklow Brow Primary School

THE GIANT'S CASTLE

Inside the giant's castle
Where the giant lives
He has a huge bed
Ten times the size of an elephant.
A big, fat, giant is his dad.
He is fifteen times bigger than him.
His hair is as spiky as a hedgehog
The giant is very, very lonely because he lives in the middle of nowhere
In the castle.

Michael Peasgood (9)
Blacklow Brow Primary School

MY TREASURE

A treasure that is mine,
Small, white and fluffy,
Who bounces all around.
I've got a tale to tell
About my little rabbit
Who died a long time ago.

One day a fox came to see
What he could find.
Something caught his eye,
Running in the distance,
He crept slowly then fast then faster . . .
Silence, my treasure has gone.

Heidi Langton (11)
Blacklow Brow Primary School

HIDDEN TREASURES

Hidden treasures, secret fears,
The things that make you burst into tears.
Jewels and diamonds to behold,
Memories like a chest of gold.

My mum and dad sat on the beach,
The entire world within my reach.
But as I let the time linger,
The memories slip through my fingers.
I wish to picture them one more time,
And if I close my eyes I will often find,
Myself in the past where I long to be
Only us, my family and me.

Amy Gilmore (10)
Blacklow Brow Primary School

MY MEMORIES

He batted the air,
And played with my hair,
He rolled on my bed,
And wrestled with my ted.

He brought us joy,
Better than any toy,
The day after my birthday,
Was when he came to stay,
And this is what I want to say.

He ran across the grass,
Tried to jump through glass,
He was black and white
He tried to give us a fright,
And stalked around in the dead of night.

He was special
But now he is gone, he is not coming back
I'll never forget him
He was my special cat.

Elizabeth Cragg (11)
Blacklow Brow Primary School

TREASURE

Treasure underneath the sea, that's where I need to be
I need to find a way down here, to see what I can see
I swim all day this is what I need to say
The sea glistened under the sun while I am having so much fun.

Victoria Smith (11)
Blacklow Brow Primary School

MY DOG KAI

My dog Kai is a lightning bolt of speed,
Anything I could do he can do ten times better,
He can run faster, jump higher,
Play football, play tug of war with me.
My dog Kai is my hidden treasure!
He's at home waiting for me,
Looking for me, his playmate.
My dog Kai is my hidden treasure!
My dog Kai is as white as snow,
He is a white, fluff ball,
On his walks he drags me round the block,
He is the strongest pup I know.
My dog Kai is my hidden treasure!

Joshua Rogers (10)
Blacklow Brow Primary School

HIDDEN TREASURES

I was under my bed,
When I banged my head,
I found my old cap
Folded by a map,
A gleaming sea,
That's what I could see,
I found my grandad's old memories in a box
I opened the box to let them shine,
Just to remember that fantastic grandad of mine.

James Hannon (10)
Blacklow Brow Primary School

VICTORIA HOUSE

Down in the cellar of Victoria House
Lives nothing more than a scurrying mouse
Or so they say, is it true?
There's no evidence, not even a clue
And as you descend the steps of doom
Darkness dominates the darkened room
But who knows? There might be something there
Maybe a ghost to encounter if you dare.
But what would it want? Why would it be here?
To encounter its visitor with echoing fear
Now I know there's more than a mouse
Down in the cellar of Victoria House!

Patrick Taft (11)
Blacklow Brow Primary School

MY HIDDEN TREASURE

You are always there for me when I've hurt myself or when I'm ill.

You cook my tea, make me hot baths and tuck me into bed.

But when I've had a really bad day you always cheer me up
in every way.

Even though you tell me off
When I grow up you will still be the world's number one mum
Forever and ever.

That's my hidden treasure to keep.

Melissa Gee (10)
Blacklow Brow Primary School

TREASURE HUNT

I'm on a treasure hunt,
To find the hidden treasure,
Buried underground, buried in the sand.
I've got a map to help me
But really it's no use.

It's hard to understand,
With pictures all around,
Will I ever find the treasure?
I will never know,
I will leave the map here,
For other people to have a go,
And find the hidden treasure.

Heather Martin (11)
Blacklow Brow Primary School

HIDDEN TREASURES

In my head lie my memories,
Of when I was two or three.
In my head lie my memories,
Of my old gran and grandad.
In my head lie my memories,
Of when it was my first birthday.
In my head lie my memories,
Of when my new brother was born.
In my head lie my memories,
Of me writing this poem.

James Lambert (10)
Blacklow Brow Primary School

HIDDEN TREASURE

Trying to find the beautiful treasure
It's locked in my head forever and ever
I've got to find the treasure,
Because it will bring me a lot of pleasure,
Where, oh where could it be?
It might be under the sea,
And it's waiting for you and me.

David Campbell (10)
Blacklow Brow Primary School

MY RABBIT

You are a banana, soft and smooth.
You are sunshine, pretty and bright.
You are a BMW, fast and smart.
You are the colour yellow, cheerful and fun.
You are party music, bouncy and fun.
You are a pillow, comfy and soft.

Stephanie Weston (8)
Blacklow Brow Primary School

MY SISTER MAYA

You are a grape, sweet and soft.
You are sunshine, calm and bright.
You are a mini, slow and small.
You are the colour yellow, cool and calm.
You are pop music, loud and lively.
You are an old couch, comfy and snug.

Connor Haddley (7)
Blacklow Brow Primary School

THE MONSTER'S CAVE

As I crept into the monster's cave
I was feeling very brave.
But suddenly a monster jumped out
And I gave a tremendous shout.

As I ran further into the cave
I was not feeling quite as brave.
My knees were shaking,
My heart was racing

The cave was dark and smelly
I tickled the monster's belly.
The monster fell down with laughter
So I ran out, straight after.

Rachael Casey (9)
Blacklow Brow Primary School

A MOTHER'S TREASURE

She is my bundle of joy,
She is my treasure forever,
She is like a candle in the dark,
All I need is her love,
She walked into my life and
Stopped my tears,
Everything is easy now,
I have her near every time she touches me I feel like a hero.

She is my treasure!

Rebecca Henry (10) & Rebecca Toulmin (9)
Blacklow Brow Primary School

LOST

Some people cry,
Some people just don't say a word,
Some people scream aloud,
But the teardrop rolls down
My face when I think of you.
You cheered me up when I was down,
You taught me how to enjoy life,
When I look at you on my photograph
All the good memories come flowing back.
So Uncle Steven if you can hear me up there
You are my hidden treasure.

Hannah Monaghan (9)
Blacklow Brow Primary School

GOLD

It beams down its golden rays
And glistens across the ocean
Like golden glitter smudged across
A deep blue page.

It bathes on fluffy, white, cotton wool balls
Surrounded by a light blue substance.

It's a pan of boiling gold dye,
Poured into a perfect circle with excess splodges.

Our hidden treasure is the glistening sun!

Catherine Marshall & Alexa Humphries (9)
Blacklow Brow Primary School

THE EXPLORER'S ATTIC

John the explorer is fifty-one,
He was dreaming of days that had gone
His brain is filled with memories and souvenirs
Of a time that was spent on different careers.
He lives in a cottage older than himself
With an attic of maps, grappling hooks, rope and other equipment
on the shelf.

In the corner is a pair of dirty, old boots
They smell like they have grown mouldy, a plant shoot.

Long-retired and ready for a rest
John in the attic is sad and not at his best
Adventures gone and only memories remain
Of American forests explored but not in vain.

Treasures around him all around the attic,
Fantastic, superb, they're rewards for being an explorer
Fantastic.

Charles Morris (9)
Blacklow Brow Primary School

DOLPHIN - WHAT IS IT?

Its silky, smooth body elegantly jumps out of the graceful ocean.

It glides through the cold, blue water looking for its baby.

It makes beautiful noises and its body is shaped like a letter N.

What is it?
A mother dolphin.

Katherine Gollicker (9) & Abbie Hooton (10)
Blacklow Brow Primary School

THE ALIEN SPACECRAFT

In the middle of nowhere
A spacecraft landed
There was nobody there
It was just as they'd planned it.

It was flying saucer-shaped
And as big as the Millennium Dome.
If I had the noises taped they'd believe me when I get home.

It landed on its tripod legs
Its coloured lights were flashing,
The aliens had two big heads
They were ugly and perfect for bashing.

Ben Knight (8)
Blacklow Brow Primary School

LFC - LIVERPOOL

Michael Owen
Is worth a poem.
Fowler's gone
But Liverpool's still number one.
Gerald Houllier has got the best team
Everton would be this good in their manager's dream.
Their fans sing songs
While they play making no wrongs.
They're the team that totally rule
So what's their name?
Liverpool.

Conal Traverse (10) & Matthew Lee (9)
Blacklow Brow Primary School

LFC

The world is spinning faster
Michael Owen's on the ball
Steven Gerrard puts a cross in
And Heskey's going to score.

But then the oaf falls over
And takes the keeper down
So Owen just sprints over
And blasts it in the crowd.

The Kop then all get angry
As they scream their awful rage
They all shout 'Transfer Owen!
But leave us with his wage.'

Jake Gillon (10)
Brookside Primary School

MONSTER ON HOLIDAY

Monster on a plane,
Monster in his room,
Monster on the beach
Playing in the sea.
Monster with his wife,
Monster on a cruise ship
Having a good time.
Monster gone asleep,
Monster drinking bleach,
Monster got the creeps,
Monster gone home.

Martine Ashworth (10)
Brookside Primary School

HAUNTED HOUSE

I went into a haunted house
The first thing I saw was a mouse,
I went upstairs and found three bears
I ran back down, saw a clown.
I got my gun out and made him frown
I went into the kitchen and saw a pigeon.
I ran into the hall and found a ball
I saw the bears and the clown
I got my gun out and shot them all down.
As I ran out of the house I saw an ugly, giant mouse
I ran into the scary wood
My feet got stuck in lots of mud.
I escaped from the wood as best as I could
As I ran across the road after me the giant mouse strode.
I jumped into a tree onto a branch that looked like me.
As I got onto a bus, the driver's hand was full of puss.
I got off the bus and bought myself a slush
As I was drinking I was also thinking
Of all the things that had happened to me.
I'd had a bad scare with that awful nightmare
No more scary movies for me.

Christopher Keefe (10)
Brookside Primary School

HEALTHY THINGS TO EAT

Vegetables and meat are good things to eat
Juice and milk are good to drink.
I really like soup, chicken's my best
Tomatoes ain't bad but I don't like the rest.

I also like spaghetti, especially on toast
It's probably what I eat the most.
Burgers and chips are also a winner
These are just a few things I have for my dinner.

Perry O'Sullivan (9)
Brookside Primary School

THE ANCIENT MARINER

T   his is the ancient mariner
H   e has a long beard and a glittering eye
E   ftsoons his skinny hand dropped the wedding guest.

A   nd he listened like a three-year-old child
'N   ow wherefore stopp'st thou me?' He said
C   alling to his dead crew
I   f only I could pray to god
E   veryone might be safe.
N   ever kill an albatross
T   he very deep did rot; slimy things did crawl with legs upon
                                                        the slimy sea.

M   ay I be forgiven
A   nd take this from my neck
R   each down for me please he cried to god
I   n this moment I am desperate
N   obody will know about this
E   ven though I still feel guilty
R   emember he prayeth well who loveth well both man, bird and beast.

Now the ship was still, as idle as a painted ship upon
                                                        a painted ocean.

Ashleigh Corrigan (11)
Eastcroft Park CP School

LOVE

I'm newly born every day in a heart,
I have a family that live all over the world,
Deep in a white, floating clouds
Wearing red, flowing robes,
Our fears are wars,
We like to make people have a soft spot for others,
We would like to make sad people jolly again.

Danielle McCarthy (10) & Victoria Royston (11)
Eastcroft Park CP School

FIRE

Fire, fire as hot as lava
Fire, fire as red as a Liverpool kit,
Fire, fire causing commotion as fast as a speeding motorbike
It screams through the sleeping town.

Thomas Caunter (11)
Eastcroft Park CP School

VOLCANO HAIKU

I'm a volcano
I never sleep, day or night
I erupt, cause fright.

Daniel Shiers (11)
Eastcroft Park CP School

WHO IS THE MARINER?

T here he has a long, tatted, grey beard
H is glittering eyes will make you fall
E ven his creepy, skinny hand may make a terrible scene for all

A nd as he left the busy harbour a wonderful cheer was heard.
N ever has he seen a worse storm
C annons of wind blew the ship from side to side
I ce was all around
E ven as the wind blew on
N ot even the strongest man wouldn't be scared
T hrough the fog came a wonderful albatross

M ariner filled with joy
A lbatross was killed with the mariner's crossbow
R ound his neck it was hung
I n the noon his crew were taken away
N ow on his own
E ven if he could pray to god
R ain might still never fall.

Jessica Weller (10)
Eastcroft Park CP School

TANKA

Tiny, sharp pencil
I always use it for work
Every single day
It is my best friend's pencil
It's very sharp and spiky.

Jamie Stokes (11)
Eastcroft Park CP School

THE PARTY

Dancing through the night
Long conversations till dawn
My auntie's party
It carried on going for twenty-four hours
Then my auntie went to bed before we woke up.

James Klieve (10)
Eastcroft Park CP School

THE DARK IS HERE

Beaming eyes, sharp sounds,
Moving shadows, talking toys
Wishing day will come
Dark goes, light comes, I am safe
What will night bring tomorrow?

Emma Rosenthal & David Myres (10)
Eastcroft Park CP School

THE MOON

The moon
Shines bright through night
The moon covers the sun
And that forms the total eclipse
Pitch-black.

Leanne Durney (10)
Eastcroft Park CP School

THE VOLCANO

The volcano was an angry giant
Shaking its fists
Its voice was a blistering marble,
Its red hair was flaming hot and crimson,
Its eyes were steaming like a hot tomato,
The smell of the volcano was terrible
It smelt like a smoke and ash.
Its rumbling and tumbling was like a smoky train squeaking.
One has just erupted
It has just turned into a fireball
They are shocking
Its skin is so rocky you could try to take the rocky rocks of the volcano
It starts to stare you away
Its eyes are yellow too
Boo, the volcano has just erupted.

Aishea Evans (10)
Eastcroft Park CP School

THE SEA

The sea is calm and clear blue
Waving at the sandy, gritty shore.

Full of life, plant or animal
Deeper than deep and darker than dark.

Gardens of coral mysterious,
Beautiful, quiet and perfect.

The sea is calm and clear blue
Waving at the sandy, gritty shore.

Alex Barry (10)
Eastcroft Park CP School

FOG

I am a grey cloak
I blanket the world like a giant blowing smoke
I fall slowly, silently, swiftly, gliding over, under and around
                                        softly swirling.

I create a misty vacuum
With my ghostly fingertip.
Endless space, eerie silence,
Making you feel alone
Tickling you with my feathery touch
Making my presence clear
I whisper in your ear
But I'm not really there.
I can be any shape or size
Transforming from location to location
I am a mysterious stranger
Full of hidden secrets.
I make everyone unknown
Especially myself.

Home 12
Eastcroft Park CP School

VOLCANO

The volcano was an angry giant shaking its fists,
Its voice like thunder pouring out of its mouth,
Its red hair swiftly covering the ground,
Its eyes burning with fiery rage,
Its smoky smell polluting the village air,
Its skin spread out like a pile of rubble.

James Bigley (11)
Eastcroft Park CP School

Dogs

Fire hogger,
Cat chaser,
Human minder,
Bone eater,
High jumper,
Fast runner,
Ankle biter,
Mad fighter,
Teddy cuddler,
Wild barker,
Shoe chewer,
Natural swimmer,
Quick learner,
Feet licker,
Bottom sniffer,
Everyone's favourite pet.

Terrylee Thomson (10)
Eastcroft Park CP School

Chocolate

Very cosy in places,
Getting softer every day,
Dancing around the streets
In a gorgeous, floaty, brown wrapper,
Like wallowing in mud . . . but smooth and delicious
Chocolate, a very close friend on a lonely, winter night.

Michelle Lawson (11)
Eastcroft Park CP School

SNOW

The snow as cold as ice
And very spongy
And it feels like cotton wool
And very bouncy and springy,
And it looks like the clouds and white as a sheet
And likes to keep cool and soft and squashy.

Natasha Williams (11)
Eastcroft Park CP School

MICHAEL OWEN

As he runs down the wing
Wind in his face,
Football in possession,
He is the ace.

Paul Fahey (10)
Eastcroft Park CP School

BEST FRIEND

Smart, caring, funny,
They are always there for you
That is a best friend.
Best friends are understanding
Sharing all your deepest thoughts.

Laura Ambrose (11)
Eastcroft Park CP School

ANGER

Anger as old as creation with a chalk white face,
Enormous, starring, bloodshot eyes piercing into his victims
Stealing away calm and control.

Anger, dressed in red and black silky robes
His limbs protruding
As though they have burst free from a straightjacket
Breathing fire and spitting liquid hot magma,
He erupts cat-like from his lava pit.

Anger, sizzling through gritted teeth
Tormenting and humiliating innocents into his trap.

Home 12
Eastcroft Park CP School

SEA SECRETS

The waves so calm, ripple to the shore
As the sun sets like an orange orb
Lighting the ocean bottom
Where the scaled fish sway to the sound of a silent tune.

Sequinned mermaids gather to watch
Seaweed dancing like leaves in the wind
Starfish mirror the twinkling stars in the darkening sky above.

The tide begins its steady rhythm in and out
Breathing like some gigantic monster
Dark blue and deep, what secrets does it keep?
As the water travels through distant lands!

Amy Holland-Rathmill (10)
Hunts Cross Primary School

DORMICE IN THE FOREST

A little mouse opens his door
Then scampers across the foggy, forest floor
He stretches and points his hands to the sky
As a silent moth passes by.

The moon shimmers through the tall trees
But no noise can be heard from the bees,
The mouse hurries to collect some berries
And on his way meets a badger eating cherries.

Lonely, the forest seems so blue
Nothing is awake except for the mouse and a hare
Everywhere is quiet, dark and still,
Then something moves underneath a leafy hill.

The mouse jumps back behind a bush
As something pops up in a rush
It knocked over a soggy, wet box
And fearfully the dormouse saw it was a fox.

Quickly he ran back to his house,
'The fox cannot get me; I'm only a mouse!'
But now dormouse is safe and sound
In his straw, he is bound.

Now the mouse is fast asleep,
He may not wake, for another week
He lays as peaceful as the forest bay,
But now animals are waking for the day.

Sarah Harrison (11)
Hunts Cross Primary School

GOLDFISH

A scaly tail
Like a mini whale.

Fast swimmer,
It's a winner.

Full of fun
As bright as the sun.

Small eyes,
Very wise.

Silky fins,
Like golden wings.

Waiting to be fed
Then sleep in its wet bed.

You guessed it
It was a goldfish
Stuck in a round dish.

Michelle Williams (10)
Hunts Cross Primary School

SNOW

Snow is as white as polar bears.
Snow is as cold as a December night.
Snow is like fluffy clouds in the blue sky.
Snow is as soft as a piece of stuffing out of a pillow.
Snow is like fur on a rabbit's coat.
Snow is as gentle as a puppy.

Emma Taylor (10)
Hunts Cross Primary School

THE PRINCESS

The sun was a mirror of dazzling gold that shone upon the seas.
The dress was a frill of silk that came down to her knees.
The red carpet was a sheet of blood flowing to her room
And the princess came dancing, dancing, dancing.
The princess came dancing to meet her handsome groom.

Kelly Maguire (10)
Hunts Cross Primary School

THE DEVIL

The storm was a treacherous thunderbolt over the village house.
The lava was a clump of fire killing even the tiniest mouse.
The moon was a shining light warding off harmful creatures
And the Devil came murdering, murdering, murdering.
The Devil came murdering up to the lair full of preachers.

Kyle Buckley (10)
Hunts Cross Primary School

THE KING'S BEAUTIFUL CROWN

The king's beautiful crown
Was so shiny and gold
But everybody in the town
Wanted a big, big hold.

The king's beautiful crown
Was so spiky and sharp
But every time he eats a prawn
He always felt like a big musical harp.

The king's beautiful crown
Was so flat and smooth
When the king said 'Come right here now!'
Everybody went - 'Move!'

Rebecca Fitzgerald (9)
Hunts Cross Primary School

THE PRINCESS OF JIGSAW ISLAND

The princess of Jigsaw Island
Went to sea one day
She sailed on a triangle dolphin
As she went on her way.

She sailed over waves
As big as a cat
She came to an island
As big as a mat.

She saw that everything
Was upside down,
Everything was happy
And no one had a frown.

'Let's go for a walk,
Have a tea party with the cats
We will visit the people and play all day.

Bye,' said the princess
As she sailed away
'I had a good time
I will come another day.'

Robyn Hannah (8)
Hunts Cross Primary School

WHAT IS IT?

Three gills,
Gives me chills.

Eats fish,
But not off a dish.

A hit in the nose,
Away it goes.

A man it will eat,
It loves lots of meat.

It's got lots of pace,
An uglier face.

It can sense in the dark,
It's a great white shark.

Ricky McDonough (11)
Hunts Cross Primary School

VOLCANO PLANET

The king of planet Earth
Had to go for a surf
He went through space
To a volcanic planet like a race.

The sun was like an oblong,
And the volcanoes make a dong
The lava's as blue as the sea,
Or sometimes as green as a pea.

The volcanoes are like giant taps,
And burned up all my maps
Volcanoes are like giant mountains,
And make some excellent fountains.

So I went back to Earth
Again having a surf
I was at last at my kingdom
Where I was served with chewing gum.

Peter Duffield (8)
Hunts Cross Primary School

A WAGGING TAIL

A wagging tail
Collects the mail.

A big eater,
Loves the heater.

Hates the cat,
Likes the mat.

Has human taste,
Hates waste.

Needs love,
Watches the dove.

We love logs,
That's what makes us dogs.

Ashley Purchase (10)
Hunts Cross Primary School

UP IN THE ATTIC

A pile of hats
In the corner,
Dirty window ledges,
Mousetrap snaps,
Little, crawly bugs,
Ugly, old bats,
Boxes filled with clothes,
Portrait that stares,
Four little spiders,
Ragged teddy bears,
Torn, white sheets,
Dusty, old chairs,
Up in the attic.

Charlotte Fitzgerald (10)
Hunts Cross Primary School

FEAR

Fear is the scorching hot flame of Hell,
The feeling you get when you're trapped in a cell.
The piercing scream that wakes you at night,
The feeling that makes you want to see the light.
The feeling that you just can't get out of your head,
It just makes you yell out 'I wish I was dead!'
You just want to get out of here,
It's the blood-curdling shrill everyone feels,
It's the worst feeling in the world
It's fear.

Alex Ashton (11)
Hunts Cross Primary School

DOWN IN THE CELLAR

Down in the cellar . . .
Old squeaky rats,
Mouldy blankets,
Dusty ragged mats,
Cobwebs all around,
Old ripped hats,
Messy black maps,
Cold stone floor,
Toys piled high
Bottles scattered by the door,
Photos of school hols,
Memories of
The seashore.

Aimee Evans (9)
Hunts Cross Primary School

DOWN IN THE CELLAR

Down in the cellar . . .
Paintings of Henrietta,
Broken bits of bed,
Torn ripped sweater,
Little spiders crawling,
Old company letter,
Cobwebs on the walls,
Pictures of the Blitz,
Dusty wedding photos,
Old toilet bits,
Sticky stone floor,
Super major,
Dark pits.

Michael Byrne (9)
Hunts Cross Primary School

DOWN IN THE CELLAR

Down in the cellar . . .
Piles of damp coal,
Creepy enormous spiders,
Dead people with no soul,
Fat ugly rats,
Rotten dark scroll,
Dusty cobwebs in the corners,
Little scary mice,
Rusty wet pipes
Stale old rice,
Sharp dagger-like tools,
And little
Haunting woodlice.

James McHugh (10)
Hunts Cross Primary School

DOWN IN THE CELLAR

Down in the cellar . . .
Where rats lay nests,
Eating on a pizza,
Where a dead body rests,
Radiators that used to work,
Spiders are a pest,
Black and white computer,
Old McDonald's box,
Wine spilt everywhere,
Selection of locks,
Big splodge of oil
Over my great
Grandad's socks.

Michelle Kelly (10)
Hunts Cross Primary School

DOWN IN THE CELLAR

Down in the cellar . . .
Where all the rats sleep,
Wine bottles broken,
Blankets in a heap,
Buckets and brushes,
Stray cats weep,
Spiders waiting to scare,
Boots that stink,
Cobwebs hanging down,
Pens that exploded with ink,
Broken clocks in the corner,
Water burst from
Battered sink.

Yolanda Hyland (9)
Hunts Cross Primary School

UP IN THE ATTIC

With stories to tell
Dusty old window,
Old toy well,
Joke book that's new,
Old doll called Mel,
Rusty bird cage,
Calendar of May,
Battered doll's cot
With rotten hay,
Old toy box,
Torn newspapers lay
Up in the attic.

Adam Saunders (10)
Hunts Cross Primary School

UP IN THE ATTIC

Horse stables
And tattered
Swinging dart boards,
Ripped clothes labels,
Old bicycle wheels,
Lay down tables,
Grandfather clocks,
Doll's house stairs,
Pieces of ornaments,
Dusty carpet hairs,
Old rocking horse,
Broken legs from chairs,
Up in the attic.

Marvin Turner (10)
Hunts Cross Primary School

UP IN THE ATTIC

With fat bellies,
Fat toy clowns,
Old footie gloves,
Old broken tellies,
Dusty old tool box,
Damp stinky wellies,
Old battered toys,
Pictures of red setters,
Rough paintings on walls
Dirty torn sweaters,
Clothes on floor,
Ragged old letters,
Up in the attic.

Ross Balmforth (9)
Hunts Cross Primary School

UP IN THE ATTIC

I must go,
I know,
Mum's old beauty mags,
Smell of clothes I know,
Deadly black bats,
Cards from years ago,
Torn up love letters,
Photos taken with a cam,
Dad's worthless tools,
Old toy lamb,
Dusty Christmas decs,
Broken doll's pram,
Up in the attic.

Katie Doran (9)
Hunts Cross Primary School

UP IN THE ATTIC

From our hols
Summer clothes,
Christmas decorations,
Haunting red-eyed trolls,
Albums of old friends,
Binbags of china dolls,
Teddy I used to cuddle,
Box of my first clogs,
Soft woollen blanket,
Moss growing on logs,
Old armchair,
Collars from my dogs,
Up in the attic.

Jennie Gervais (9)
Hunts Cross Primary School

THE ISLAND OF CHATTERING ANIMALS AND THE QUEEN

When I got on the boat
I had a sore throat
I could not talk for a while
But we have only sailed a mile.

I saw a blue and purple crocodile
That was as big as my feet
And every time I went near it
I nearly was dead meat.

I saw a little fish
Swimming in the sea
What really freaked me out
Was the way it looked at me.

Rachel Bird (9)
Hunts Cross Primary School

IN THE NIGHT

At midnight tonight there was nothing to be heard,
The sky was so cloudy that it started to get blurred,
Raindrops battered the ground making it the loudest sound.

The rain had stopped and the clouds passed by
The moonlight galloped across the sky
The sky that bright just like an electric light.

All the night started to run because they were having so much fun
Rabbits roamed round and round,
Badgers beavered, burrowing into the ground.

Peter Burke (11)
Hunts Cross Primary School

THE SPOOKY WOODS

Down in the woods
Shines the shimmering moon
Round and fat
Like a golden balloon.

The trees crouch down
With thin grabbing hands
They shout out loud
Across the misty lands.

They stir, they look,
With their beady eyes
The wind blows,
And slowly cries.

Chelsey Grosart (11)
Hunts Cross Primary School

SNOW

Snow is as white as a piece of paper.
Snow is as soft as a pillow.
Snow is as twinkling as the moon.
Snow is as glowy as the stars in the sky.

Snow is as calm as a sleeping dog.
Snow is as light as a feather.
Snow is like raindrops from the sky.
Snow is as nice as a warm fire.

Stephanie Harrald (9)
Hunts Cross Primary School

THE SEA

The sea is as cool as ice.
The sea is as blue as the sky.
The sea is as fierce as a lion.
The sea is as salty as salt.
The sea is as calm as white, fluffy clouds.
The sea is as big as an elephant.
The sea is as sparkling as a star.

Isabel Collings (9)
Hunts Cross Primary School

SNOW

Snow is as soft as a pillow.
Snow is as white as clouds.
Snow is as cold as a fridge freezer.
Snow is as slow as a snail.
Snow is as calm as an ant.
Snow is as fun as a playground.

Paul Evans (10)
Hunts Cross Primary School

THE ALIEN

The sky was a dark bat flying over the trees.
The sun was a dark fireball above the seas.
The stream was a squiggly road rushing on its way
And the alien came hovering, hovering, hovering.
And the alien came hovering down to the subway.

Ryan Cornfoot (10)
Hunts Cross Primary School

THE FOOTIE PLAYER

The boots were thunderbolts scoring up to Heaven.
The kit was a shining star with lucky number seven.
The tunnel was a dark cave coming out into the light
And the footie player came jogging, jogging, jogging.
The footie player came jogging up to the centre with all his might.

Luke Forsyth (10)
Hunts Cross Primary School

THE GHOSTLY SOUL

The sky was a blast of darkness that reaped across the town.
The moon was a bright sphere that had the face of a clown.
The stream was a never-ending snake that flowed across the moor
And the ghostly soul came limping, limping, limping.
The ghostly soul came limping up to the old castle door.

Samantha Foster (10)
Hunts Cross Primary School

THE PHANTOM PLAYER

The moon was a football shimmering in the light.
The sky was a black sheet in the night.
The grass was a smooth carpet spreading around
And the phantom player came dribbling, dribbling, dribbling.
The phantom player came dribbling up to the massive mound.

Thomas Musa (10)
Hunts Cross Primary School

THE GHOSTLY NIGHT TRAIN

The sky was a sheet of darkness above the misty tracks.
The rain was a pouring bucket on all the people with macs.
The track was a slimy snake slithering through the town
And the ghostly night train came chugging, chugging, chugging,
The ghostly night train came chugging up to the old, wooden clown.

Molly Dolan (9)
Hunts Cross Primary School

THE GHOST TRAIN

The sky was a pearl of blue among the ghostly trees.
The moon was a sparkling star shining on the seas.
The track was a metal snake creeping in the town
And the ghost train came tooting, tooting, tooting,
The ghost train came tooting up to the ghost with a frown.

Sarah Jones (10)
Hunts Cross Primary School

THE UNICORN

The rain was a million bullets falling from the sky.
The cloud was a shield of darkness forming way up high.
The stream was a slithering snake bending on its way
And the unicorn came galloping, galloping, galloping.
The unicorn came galloping up to the windy bay.

Neil Skidmore (9)
Hunts Cross Primary School

BLUEBERRY FOREST

Beyond the gate of the Blueberry Forest
The distant whistle of a wolf springs by
The leaf-carpeted floor shimmers upon the night sky
Webby trees fill the wind-broken forest.

The trunk of the old oak sways from side to side
The little dormouse has nowhere to hide
Beaten upon their track the owls are looking for a tasty snack
The moon shines down on the forest and fills it with silence . . .

Rachael Jennings (11)
Hunts Cross Primary School

A FISH

One small fish in a polythene bag
Can't swim round can only look sad.
Take a pair of scissors
Snip a quick hole.
Down flops water and fish into a bowl.
She waits a little moment
Flips her tail free.
Then off into circles
As frisky as can be.
Dash-about, splash-about,
Do what you will, you're mine
You black-spotted, cheeky-eyed fish.

Nikki Walsh (7)
Mab Lane Primary School

HEAD OFF BY HENRY

Henry the Eight is my name
It wasn't my fault my wives were to blame.
Moaning and whining they drove me insane
I chopped off their heads like a horse's mane.
My first was Catherine of Aragon
Now she was Spanish, so seriously annoying I said all gone.
Next up was Anne Boleyn
Sadly though she could not win.
After that was poor Jane Seymour
It was even worse she couldn't see me more.
We had a little boy and named him Edward
He's the king now
And I'm ending this poem as I take my last bow.

Ashley Spencer (10)
Mab Lane Primary School

THE HOLIDAY

Come to Liverpool, bright and breezy
Stay with us, it's free and easy.
Lovely bedrooms, home-cooked nosh,
Cosy, friendly, nothing posh.
Close to Liverpool's private beach
Shows and shops in easy reach.

Michael Bishop (10)
Mab Lane Primary School

JUNGLE FEVER

Jungle fever hit me like a bolt of lightning
The lion is coming
Help it's coming near me
I'll get away but I'll run very fast
Through the bright, green bushes.
I'll be camouflaged
I can get away very fast
I've fallen
There is a snake right in front of me
Yes, I've got away.

Danielle Fanning (10)
Mab Lane Primary School

A PLEASANT DREAM

I lay dreaming of playing for Liverpool
Up I ran, looking cool.
Always looking back
Eventually I turned so I could keep track.
Every time the crowd went wild
What an imagination for a child.
I was number nine
And looking fine.
I had a shot.
Goal!

Jonathan Bridgeman (10)
Mab Lane Primary School

CRAZY COMET

Shooting silver just like stars
Where is it coming from the moon or Mars?
Flashing lights in the sky
Just like a streamer passing by.
Where it comes from no one knows
But one thing's for sure
It makes one spectacular show.

Erin Fitzgerald (10)
Plantation Primary School

THE BURGLAR

The burglar's coming
He's been before
He took some stuff
And he wants some more.

He's broken the window,
He's smashed the door,
And knocked Mum's flowers
All over the floor.

He looks around and
Grabs some swag,
He puts it all in
His great, big bag.

Then out the window
And past the door,
Oh dear!
He's bumped right into
The law!

Louise Close (8)
St Aloysius RC Primary School

ILLNESS

Illness is khaki,
It tastes like vomit,
It smells like sewage,
It looks like a polluted water hole.
Illness sounds like nails scratching a blackboard.
Illness suffocates me.

Illness is pea-green,
It tastes sour,
It smells like garbage,
It looks like a slimy snake.
Illness sounds like a burp.
Illness hurts me.

Illness is sludge green,
It tastes horrible,
It smells like factory fumes,
It looks like a blob of goo.
Illness sounds like a raging storm.
Illness frustrates me.

Anthony Lynch (11)
St Aloysius RC Primary School

FRUSTRATION

Frustration is smoky,
It tastes like pea-green lollipop,
It looks like a shadow and
Smells like vomit,
It feels like rough hands.

Joseph Kennedy (11)
St Aloysius RC Primary School

MY BROTHER SHAUN

My brother Shaun is a nuisance,
He messes my room and
I get the blame.
He likes to throw his toys at me,
It makes him laugh and me cry.

My brother Shaun wakes me up
By bouncing on my bed
And my head.
He takes the food off my plate
When I'm not looking.

My brother Shaun
Never lets me watch the TV
In peace, he thinks it's more fun
To switch it off during the most
Exciting part.

My brother Shaun is a nuisance.
But my brother Shaun is brave,
He has needles twice a day
Just because he has a thing called diabetes.

My brother Shaun is a nuisance
But I love him . . . that's for sure.

Daniel Midghall (9)
St Aloysius RC Primary School

I LOVE FOOTBALL

I love football, it's really great
But not for girls
It's too rough for girls.
I scored six goals this week

Last week I scored a hat-trick
And my team won.
I love football, it's really great
I'm going to play for Liverpool one day.

Jason Welsh (8)
St Aloysius RC Primary School

LOOKING THROUGH MY WINDOW

Looking through my window, what do I see?
A cat with large green eyes
Staring back at me.
I go to turn away, then I heard him call my name
'Come and play Becky, I know an exciting game.'
I think I've lost my marbles,
I think I've lost my mind.
I've never heard a cat speak,
A cat of any kind.
In a frightened voice I shout,
'Please, please go away.'
But the cat just smiled strangely
And replied, 'Oh please just come and play.'
Curious I put on my woolly coat and hat
And off I went to investigate this strange, magical cat.
I rushed downstairs and outside
Into the moonlit night.
Looking for the cat that sat under
The cold street light.
But to my disappointment the cat had gone it seemed.
It must have been a vision one, that I had dreamed.

Rebecca Fitzsimmons (8)
St Aloysius RC Primary School

LOVE

Love is a warm baby-pink,
It tastes like honeysuckle,
It smells like the air after a storm.
Love looks like a blossom tree in spring,
It sounds like a thousand children's laughter.
Love makes me feel like dancing on clouds.

Beth Campbell (11)
St Aloysius RC Primary School

ANGER

Anger is red,
It tastes like burnt chilli
And smells like fire.
Anger looks like flames,
Sounds like Satan.
Anger burns me.

Shaun Flanagan (10)
St Aloysius RC Primary School

LOVE

Love is red,
It tastes like fireballs
And smells like hot fire.
Love looks like a red rose,
The sound of two hearts pounding.
Love is sweet.

Jenny Courtney (11)
St Aloysius RC Primary School

FRUSTRATION

Frustration is a dull grey,
It smells like defeat,
It looks like a river of bubbling lava,
It sounds like Hell.
Frustration hurts me.

Jake Parr (10)
St Aloysius RC Primary School

THE STORM

The storm arrived in the middle of night,
Its force so strong it gave everyone a fright.
The wind howling like a dog in distress,
Terrified, I tucked my knees in my dress.
The lightning blazing, hurt my eyes,
I screamed for my mum, she never heard my cries.
Then the rain hit the window like a marching army,
All I could think of, this storm is driving me *barmy!*

Rebecca Campbell (8)
St Aloysius RC Primary School

ANGER

Anger is deep red,
It tastes like hot chilli and it smells like sour mustard.
Anger looks like monsters punching you.
Anger sounds like the beats of someone's finger snapping,
It makes me feel mad.

Francis Baker (10)
St Aloysius RC Primary School

LOVE

Love is a rose red,
It tastes like butterflies in your stomach,
It smells of sweet perfume.
Love sounds like a pounding heart,
It sounds like angels' wings softly swaying,
It makes a tingly feeling inside me.

Jemma Hardman (10)
St Aloysius RC Primary School

JOY

Joy is blue,
It tastes like the fruitiness of an ice lolly
And smells like blueberries.
Joy looks like a bright sun,
It is the sound of birds.

Joy makes me tingle!

Anthony Corness (10)
St Aloysius RC Primary School

ANGER

Anger is deep red,
It tastes like burnt toast,
It smells like burning wood.
Anger looks like fire.
Anger sounds like screaming.

Anger makes me mad.

Christopher Henshall (9)
St Aloysius RC Primary School

LOVE IS CRAZY

Love is wine red,
It tastes like jam in a doughnut.
Love smells like red roses,
It looks like a bright heart,
It sounds like jolly birds singing.

Love relaxes me.

Adam Lonergan (11)
St Aloysius RC Primary School

LOVE

Love is crimson red,
It tastes like toffee apples
And smells like flowers.
Love looks like a bright rose,
It sounds like birds singing.
Love is sweet.

Lyndsay Evans (10)
St Aloysius RC Primary School

ANGER

Anger is red,
It tastes like chillies,
It smells like hot peppers.
Anger looks like a volcano,
It sounds like a grunt.
Anger kills me.

Michael Wong (11)
St Aloysius RC Primary School

DANGER

Danger is as red as a chilli,
It tastes like the dentist's needle going into your gum,
It smells like gas escaping from a tank,
It looks like someone getting stabbed,
It sounds like police sirens,
It feels like your whole body's on fire.
Danger makes me cringe.

Joseph O'Neill (9)
St Aloysius RC Primary School

LOVE

Love is pink,
It tastes like ice cream,
It smells of fresh flowers.
Love looks like swans swimming around.
Love sounds like birds singing with me,
It makes me feel special inside.

Darcy Slade (9)
St Aloysius RC Primary School

LONELINESS

Loneliness is blue,
It tastes like bitter poison
And smells of oceans and tears.
Loneliness looks like a dark, deep cave,
The sound of whales being killed.
Loneliness is solitude.

Amy Hawkens (11)
St Aloysius RC Primary School

IN MY UPSIDE-DOWN WORLD

In my upside-down world
Cats run after dogs,
Children behave like adults
And adults behave like children.

In my upside-down world
Hot is cold and cold is hot.
Birds swim and fish fly,
The sky is the sea.

In my upside-down world
I am you and you are me
What an utterly amazing place to be.

Ryan Fitzpatrick (8)
St Aloysius RC Primary School

MY BIRTHDAY

My birthday was great
I had a big cake with candles
And chocolate-flavoured icing.
My birthday was brilliant,
My friends came and brought me presents.
I got rollerblades, colouring books,
But best of all I got a pogo stick.
I bounced and bounced and bounced
Until I was sick.
My birthday was the best.

Melissa Mountaine (8)
St Aloysius RC Primary School

IN THE DARK

Things are different in the dark,
Shadows become strange creatures
That try to scare me away.
The wallpaper in my bedroom
Comes alive with a thousand faces
Staring and laughing.
Under my bed, toys come alive
And try to grab my feet
As I jump quickly onto my bed.
The porcelain dolls that in daylight
Sit prettily on my shelf
Become ugly, their smiles become frowns.
In the dark things *are* different
I can't wait for the daylight.

Jamie-Leigh Stockton (9)
St Aloysius RC Primary School

THE BEACH

Strolling through the pebbled sand,
I feel the heat beneath my feet.
The sun, a golden ball
Rests gently in the sky.
The wind caresses my shoulder
And gently whispers in my ear.
The foaming sea reaches out
Its long arms inviting me to join an unknown land
Yet I stand still with the heart beneath my feet.

Lauren Corness (8)
St Aloysius RC Primary School

I WISH . . .

I wish I could stroll through the clouds
Which hang like giant snowdrops
From the ever-changing sky.
I wish I could run up the highest mountain
And like a bird of prey fly down again
Down,
Down,
Down
Swooping, gliding, floating
In the cool breeze of pine-scented air.
I wish I could swim beneath the waves,
Deeper and deeper and back again,
Like a neon fish
With their colours like jewels of
Red, blue, yellow and green.
I wish, I wish a thousand times I wish.
Will my wishes ever come true?

Megan Hopwood (8)
St Aloysius RC Primary School

LITTLE BIRD

I am a little bird, I love to fly high,
So high in the clear blue sky.
I like to watch the animals below
The rabbits, dogs, the horses, all running by.
I love the park where the children play,
The old ladies give me bread
As the ducks quack loudly, jealous.
I am a little bird.

Sean Owens (9)
St Aloysius RC Primary School

MY DREAMS

I have wonderful dreams
Where I go to faraway places,
Last week I went to Spain
And played in the pool
It was cooooool!
I meet strange people in my dreams
Of all shapes and sizes,
Some are green and red.
In my dreams I drive sports cars
And everyone stops and stares.
In my dreams I jump out of
Aeroplanes and drive out of boats.
My dreams are fun.

Louis Harpur (8)
St Aloysius RC Primary School

HOMELESS

The street is dark now apart from the moon
Its bluish-white face high in the inky sky
Lights up a doorway . . .
My doorway.
Cold and damp I search for the remains of a chocolate bar
Left in the gutter by a young child.
It's been a long day, begging
Watching a thousand faces go by.
I curl up in a ball . . . in my doorway
Covering myself with a half ripped blanket
I close my eyes, I pray for sleep.

Megan Birchall (8)
St Aloysius RC Primary School

OH WHAT A WONDERFUL WORLD

People often tell me the things that are important
Things like money, clothes, computers,
But to me life, health, love and happiness are important.
Things that we often take for granted,
Our lives could be so much nicer and safer
If we could love, respect and look after
Things that mean so much more,
Like family, friends and neighbours.
What a better world it would be if
We just took time to think about our actions.
Oh I will just keep on dreaming about a perfect world.
One day my dreams may come true
Oh what a wonderful world it could be.

Charlotte Kelly (8)
St Aloysius RC Primary School

THE WIND

Up in the sky and down the lane,
I hear the wind call my name.
Swirling up and in the air,
The noisy wind who never cares.
Over the field and down the lane,
I still hear you call my name.
Sometimes I wonder can I hide,
Or will he find me even inside.
My life would never be the same,
If I never heard the wind call my name.

Katherine McLachlan (8)
St Aloysius RC Primary School

SOMEONE I KNOW . . .

I know someone who can move his ears and move his hair at the
same time.

I know someone who can point his finger out like a gun and presses
it down and it makes a click sound.

I know someone who can bend backwards and can do funny dances.

I know someone who can jump a five foot fence and is very good
at wrestling.

I know someone who can get his tongue and touch it on his own nose.

And that someone is me!

Richard Grierson (10)
St Aloysius RC Primary School

IN MY UPSIDE-DOWN WORLD

In my upside-down world
The clock ran up the mouse,
The hill ran up Jack and Jill,
Red Riding Hood ate the wolf,
The moon jumped over the cow.

In my upside-down world,
The wolf chases the pigs,
The pigs blew the houses down.

In my upside-down,
Truly, madly, world.

Katherine Clarke (10)
St Aloysius RC Primary School

I KNOW SOMEONE . . .

I know someone who can blow bubbles out of their eyes.

I know someone who can make a donkey fly.

I know someone who cannot peal an orange.

I know someone who cannot set a picnic table up.

I know someone who cannot set a table out.

I know someone who can scream like a girl.

I know someone who can touch their nose with their tongue.

I know someone who can sleep for England.

And that someone is me.

Sophie Lamont (10)
St Aloysius RC Primary School

I KNOW SOMEONE . . .

I know someone who can touch their nose with their tongue.

I know someone who can climb in a window.

I know someone who can talk like Goofy.

I know someone who can do the splits.

I know someone who can do a back flip.

I know someone who can do funny faces.

Stephen Farrell (10)
St Aloysius RC Primary School

I KNOW SOMEONE . . .

I know someone who can set up a picnic.

I know someone who can't throw a ball.

I know someone who can say the alphabet backwards.

I know someone who would put their hands in magites.

I know someone who can do the belly ripple.

I know someone who can make their ears wiggle.

I know someone who can do the splits.

I know someone who can make their little toe wiggle.

I know someone who robs pens and pencils.

I know someone who has a bad attitude.

I know someone who is rubbish in goal.

Charlotte Hughes (10)
St Aloysius RC Primary School

I KNOW SOMEONE . . .

I know someone who can twist his arm right around.

I know someone who can lick his nose.

I know someone who can blow raspberries from his arm.

And that someone is me!

Christopher McCormick (10)
St Aloysius RC Primary School

THE BUZZY BEE

Hey! You! Come with me
We're all going to The Buzzy Bee!
Come on, hit the road,
When you get there you will have a fright,
You'll love it so much,
You will be staying all night!

So hey! You! Come with me
We're all going to The Buzzy Bee!

Hey! You! Are you trying to be funny?
Why are you eating all that honey?

You can party and dance,
So hey! You! You talking to me?
We're all going to The Buzzy Bee.

Sarah-Jane Carr (9)
St Anthony Of Padua Primary School

THE SHARK

I swam under the sea, there were dancing crabs and dancing fish
There was a shark that scared them all away
They never came back until the very next day.
I punched it in the nose, it swam away, so I went to see it the next day,
But it wasn't there, then I turned around then I saw it again.
It tried to bite me but it missed, I scared it away,
Then all of the crabs and fishes danced again after all.

Joseph Carroll (9)
St Anthony Of Padua Primary School

HIDDEN TREASURES

Down in the seabed, where nobody goes
I thought I'd go and check it out
Splash! I jumped in, the water was cold as ice
The fish, the bubbles and seaweed too.

The thing that caught my eye the most
Was a shiny dark scroll inside a long tube
I got it, I opened it and followed what it said
In deeper, I felt a hard surface, land.

I grabbed the chest and swam back up and this is what I said
'Down in the seabed where nobody goes
I thought I'd go and check it out
Splash! I jumped in, the water was as cold as ice
The fish, the bubbles and seaweed too!'

Kathryn Omar (9)
St Anthony Of Padua Primary School

RECYCLING RAP

Come and start recycling,
It's the only way,
We have got to start now or we shall have to pay,
It's best if we start now 'cause soon it will be May.

Listen to me children, hear what I say,
We have got to start recycling and save the future day,
So come on children, we have got to do it now,
If it doesn't ever happen we'll end up in a row.

Come on children, do it if you please,
Do it now and get down on your knees.
Recycling things can make some treasure,
Where it stops there's no measure!

Joseph Davis (10)
St Anthony Of Padua Primary School

HIDDEN TREASURES

Down in the dark, deep blue sea
Where no one goes except for me
I want to have a look at a ship below
But there's a big, grey shark so I don't know.

I wonder if there's any treasure down there
But then again I just don't care
I want to look
But not in an old school book
I want to stare
But I don't want to be fair
All I want is to be there
Looking at the ship down there
But where?

I'm going down
And I won't drown
I can swim
But what if I don't win.
Someone might already be there
But then again I just don't care.
I'll get it
With my diving kit
And I will always get there
In my little fast boat, but where?

Charlotte Kelly (10)
St Anthony Of Padua Primary School

HIDDEN TREASURE

The hidden treasure is under the sea
In a big, heavy chest just for me.
I hope I'll find it when I look
I have found a map in my big book.

I'll go off in my submarine
I might find it
I might not
I hope I find it when I'm out
If I don't I might shout.

In my submarine I'll go
Down in the sea very, very low
I might find my hidden treasure
If I do I'm very clever.

Think of the pleasure
I would get
If I found that treasure
Some day yet
I will.

Georgina Hoyle (10)
St Anthony Of Padua Primary School

THE DEEP BLUE SEA

The sea is something gentle
That glides with glee
That's everything like me.

The sea is something so blue
It's just like the sky
I can never say goodbye.

The sea is something cool
It's just like the pool
That's why I think it's so cool.

The sea is as blue as my eyes
Just like a dolphin that splashes in the sea
Swimming along happily.

Siobhan White (10)
St Anthony Of Padua Primary School

HIDDEN TREASURE

Splash! I'm in the sea, cold water all around me,
No air to breathe, bottomless sea filled with water,
I breathe loudly, how nervous I am!
Crowd of fishes everywhere,
But I don't really care, because there is supposed to be treasure!

A shark swims passed,
I wonder how long it will last,
I'm very still . . . it loses interest,
I think about going back
I carry on . . .

I see the shipwreck, I hurry down
Shining, glittery treasure all for me,
I pull out a strong sack out of my pack,
Fill it with treasure and hurry back.

As I get nearer, I see the light
I fill up with excitement and hurry up,
At last, I can take off my mask,
Aaaaah, I can breathe again.

Adam Ward Thomas (10)
St Anthony Of Padua Primary School

THE NEW BABY

Mum's having a baby
And I don't like it.

It will kick and bawl and scream,
It will keep us up all night,
It will take up all the space,
And it will cost more money than we think.

Mum's having a baby
And I don't like it.

It is being born next week,
And I *can* wait,
Why does it have to be me?
I had already got two brothers.

Mum's having a baby
And I don't like it.

It will be a nightmare except it's true,
'The world is in danger!' I shout.

Mum's having a baby
And I don't like it!

Thomas Sewell (10)
St Anthony Of Padua Primary School

BENEATH THE SEA

Beneath the sea is a hidden chest,
Filled with lots of treasure.

Beneath the sea is a hidden chest,
Glittering gold and silver.

Beneath the sea is a hidden chest,
Just waiting to be found.

Beneath the sea is a hidden chest,
Two divers came swimming by
And shouted for joy when they spied the treasure chest.
Hiding beyond the seaweed.

Beneath the sea is an empty treasure chest.

Kathryn Walby (9)
St Anthony Of Padua Primary School

THE SEA

The sea is a fizzy drink
Chewing away the rocks.
The sea is a giant's bubble bath
Filled with sinking sand.
The sea is melted metal,
When the sun shines upon it.
The sea is multicoloured ink,
Mixed together in an enormous sink.

The sea is full of creatures,
Fish mouths are blowing,
Big eyes are glowing,
With shiny rainbow scales.
The splashing water rippling,
Blue-gold flickering
Of slippy, slimy tails.

The sea is a blue lagoon,
Glistening in the light of the moon.
The crest of the waves,
Riding high above the sea.
I am on the seashore,
They come dancing towards me.

Alexandra Mealand (9)
St Anthony Of Padua Primary School

THE QUAFFLE

The Quaffle is red
The same as blood
It can fly in the sky
Over the wood.

It is good for playing Quidditch
It is great for a game
If you hit anyone
You're sure to get the blame.

There is a Golden Snitch
Which is surely the best
There is the Quaffle
Which is easier than the rest.

The Bludger, the worst
Which definitely hurts
Which might knock off
Your scarlet shirts.

The Quaffle you hit
In three different hoops
Slytherin, Gryffindor, Ravenclaw and
Hufflepuff
Are the four groups.

Matthew Boyes (9)
St Anthony Of Padua Primary School

THE WIND

In spring the wind is just a breeze,
In summer all the same,
In autumn the wind is quite strong,
In winter the same again.

The wind is strong and powerful,
It blows some trees down,
So now you know about the wind,
And one thing it blows down.

Rachael O'Hare (7)
St Joseph's Primary School

DOWN IN THE CELLAR

Down in the cellar where no one had been
I decided to go down there to see if it was clean.

As I thought it was not clean at all
It was very spooky with cobwebs on the wall.

But then I started to get the creeps
When I saw lots of things in great big heaps.

Then I looked down on the ground
And saw giant footprints all around.

I was very scared but wanted to know
Where the footprints led and decided to go.

So I jumped off the very last stair
And followed the footprints pair by pair.

I followed the tracks for quite a while
Until suddenly I fell upon a pile.

You would not believe what I found there
Lots of gold and plenty to share.

Katie McLoughlin (8)
St Joseph's Primary School

EXCUSES! EXCUSES!

'Excuses! Excuses!
You're late again!'
'Sorry sir, I was up all night
With cousin Jane.
When walking to school
I fell in a pool
I feel such a fool.'
'Go and dry off
Or you'll have a cough
Then tomorrow we'll see
If you can be
Early and dry.
I don't know why
You fell in a pool
On your way to school.'

Hayley Brennan (7)
St Joseph's Primary School

MY HOLIDAY DREAM

Far across the Caribbean Sea
Was an enchanted island
Untouched by destructive humans
In the valleys between a blanket
Or rich green trees were trickling springs
And fields with golden crops.
The air was full of calming sounds
Of whispering voices and twanging music
That gave endless joy.

Kate Graham (10)
St Margaret Mary's Junior School

THERE'S NO SUCH WORD AS CAN'T

A dog can't act like Arnold Schwarznegger in a drama film.
My rubber can't rub me out so I'm invisible.
Seven tulips can't persuade my teacher that we don't have to
                                             go to school
But my mum can make the best roast dinner in the world.

A whale can't do the limbo thirty inches off the floor.
Your cup can't fill up like a ghost is filling it.
Twelve blizzards can't blow the moon into the Atlantic
But my friend can run like a cheetah.

An eagle can't sing the top ten like S Club 7.
Our bed can't fly us to Jupiter like a spaceship.
Twenty-five aliens can't take over the sun
But I can run to school in five minutes.

Matthew Doyle (9)
St Margaret Mary's Junior School

TWICE UPON A TIME I SAW . . .

One ostentatious orang-utan, outgrowing,
Two tempered telephones, tendering,
Three thermostatic thighs, thrashing,
Four favourable fungi, feinting,
Five ferocious fibreglasses, fiddling,
Six subconscious sausages, subdividing,
Seven stupendous subjunctives, subdividing,
Eight equatorial epigrams, escalating,
Nine gnashing newcomers, nesting,
Ten treacherous telegrams, tempting.

Philip Hynes (9)
St Margaret Mary's Junior School

MAGIC BOX

I will put in the box . . .
The eye of a dragon,
The pot of gold at the end of a rainbow,
The inner core of the universe,
The crown of the Queen Mother.

I will put in the box . . .
The biggest planet in the world,
The wing of dragons,
The fur of a leopard,
The one and all God.

My box is fashioned from the flesh of a jaguar
The lid made from crystal and steel in the corner
The hinges are made from the horns of a bull
And the lock is made from the jaws of a shark.
I shall ride a bull in the box and eat as much food as I can in my box
I shall ride a shark in my box,
I shall swim in the sea.

Sam Murphy (10)
St Margaret Mary's Junior School

THERE'S NO SUCH WORD AS CAN'T

A rabbit can't walk like us on two feet.
My pen can't do the Okey-Kokey.
My five buttercups can't play bat and ball with their petals
But my brother Paul can make the biggest mess in the world.

A goldfish can't eat a shark.
Your knife and fork can't dance together at a ball.
Sixteen rainbows can't make the world in different colours
But my friend Hannah can sing the top twenty really badly.

A butterfly can't lay a thousand eggs for me.
Our cushions can't have a disco road on Saturday night.
Twenty-five Martians can't sing Happy Earthday to me
But I can sing the bestest songs in the world.

Jennifer Southern (8)
St Margaret Mary's Junior School

THIS IS THE ROOM

This is the room that Jack needs.

This is the door that leads to
The room that Jack needs.

This is the dad behind the door
That leads to the room
That Jack needs.

This is the sister who is pushing past Jack
And is giving the door an almighty thwack
And is saying to Dad, 'It can't take that long to shave a chin.'

This is the chin being shaved
By the dad who is behind the door
That leads to the room that Jack needs.

This is the dog, all hairy and brown
Who jumps on Jack and knocks him down
And covers his face with a million licks
And doesn't stop till it's given a kick.

This is the puddle on the carpet outside the door
And this is the dad who carried out the door
And has just finished shaving now
Here comes Mum and she is asking what all the noise is about.

Hannah Maher (9)
St Margaret Mary's Junior School

THE MAGIC BOX

I will put in the box . . .
The sprinkles of a waterfall,
The fur of a wild striped tiger,
The head of a dinosaur,
The tonsils of a dragon.

I will put in the box . . .
The boiling, brightness of a fireball
The darkest eclipse ever,
The magic, softest feather of a dove,
The roar of an anxious lion.

My box is fashioned by . . .
Dolphin's fins as the sides,
Cheetah's spots as the lid,
Rat's eyes as the lock.

I will swim with dolphins
In the Atlantic Ocean and
Never come home.

Claire Cameron (9)
St Margaret Mary's Junior School

THERE'S NO SUCH WORD AS CAN'T

An elephant can't write a book like Jacqueline Wilson.
My fountain pen can't jiggle on a star.
Five roses can't do cartwheels like a clown
But my nan can make the nicest bacon butties in the world.

A starfish can't drive a car.
Your kettle can't score a goal like Michael Owen.
Sixteen raindrops can't make a lady out of confetti
But my best friend Jennifer can have the best sleepovers.

A butterfly can't get a date with Robbie Fowler.
Our bed can't do the Macarena.
Twenty-four spaceships can't come to my birthday party
But I can be a dancer on stage.

Hannah Maloney (8)
St Margaret Mary's Junior School

MEET THE WEATHER

'I am rain,
I make the world as dull as homework,
I patter on windows.'

'I am wind,
I steal hats off people's heads,
I blow trees over the road.'

'I am fog,
I trip people over,
I make houses look like spooky castles.'

'We are thunder and lightning
I sound like falling rocks,
I make your room dark.'

'I am rainbow,
I make you happy,
I show off when I come out.'

'I am snow,
I am as white as swans' feathers,
I melt in your hand.'

'I am sunshine,
I make your skin peel,
I am as hot as a million fires.'

Anthony Silvano (8)
St Margaret Mary's Junior School

MEET THE WEATHER

'I am rain,
I tap on your window sill,
I put my cold fingers on you.'

'I am wind,
I blow away your washing,
I use my terrible force on the trees.'

'I am fog,
I am as grey as a school jumper,
I am as thick as soup.'

'We are thunder and lightning,
I crash over your house,
I flash at your window.'

'I am rainbow,
I am bright as a sunny sky,
I am colourful as a picture.'

'I am snow,
I am as cold as an icicle,
I am as white as a penguin's belly.'

'I am sunshine,
I am as light as the beach,
I am brighter than one thousand lightbulbs.'

Aaron Murphy (8)
St Margaret Mary's Junior School

MY SECRET HOUSE

My house is at the edge of the forest,
It is made of white clouds.
My house is painted with starlight,
It is as cosy as a furry rabbit.

My secret pet is a ferret with sharp teeth,
Together we drink Coca-Cola.
When I'm in my house I feel cold.
My house is as wonderful as the fair.

Robyn Mulvoy (8)
St Margaret Mary's Junior School

MEET THE WEATHER

'I am rain,
I tickle against the window,
I slither down your collar.'

'I am wind,
I brush the leaves across the floor,
I fill the sea with white horses.'

'I am fog,
I make buildings look like castles,
I am as grey as the road.'

'We are thunder and lightning,
I look like sharp fingernails,
I lock you up in school.'

'I am rainbow,
I am as colourful as a peacock,
I make people happy.'

'I am snow,
I am as white as a polar bear,
Collect me and make me into a man.'

'I am sunshine,
I can blind you,
I am hotter than five hundred lightbulbs.'

Ann Power (7)
St Margaret Mary's Junior School

MAGIC BOX

I will put in the box . . .
The crashing of a waterfall,
The colours of a rainbow,
The sparkling water in summer,
The sparkle of a crystal.

I will put in the box . . .
A twinkle of a tiger's eye,
The legs of a spider,
The roar of a wolf,
The shining of the sun.

My box is fashioned from gold and silver crystals,
With shooting stars and the moon shining bright,
Its lock is a tongue hanging down from a lion.

I shall play in my box and fly
In the sky with the wind blowing
Down my top.

Adam Dixon (10)
St Margaret Mary's Junior School

THERE'S NO SUCH WORD AS CAN'T

A bird can't write a story.
My ruler can't sing.
Our flowers can't prance around
But my sister can dance like a fairy.

A fish can't go to school.
My rubber can't say hello.
My cat can't read a story
But my cousin can laugh like a hyena.

A rabbit can't talk.
A pencil can't wiggle its ears.
A pig can't dance
But my nan can cook my roast dinner like an angel.

Steffie Connell (8)
St Margaret Mary's Junior School

WONDERFUL WORLD

If black and white
Could unite
What a wonderful world it would be.

If good and bad
Was not sad
What a wonderful world it would be.

If empty and full
Was not so dull
What a wonderful world it would be.

If happy and sad
Was all you had
What a wonderful world it would be.

If slim and fat
Was not all that
What a wonderful world it would be.

If the world was divided equally
What a wonderful world it would be!

Kayleigh Blackburn (10)
St Margaret Mary's Junior School

11TH SEPTEMBER 1991

On the day that I was born
It was raining Liverpool kits from yellow clouds
Kylie Minogue made up a song about me
200 Pepsi-swigging polar bears came to my Christening
All the babies in the universe stopped crying for a week
And the man on the moon had a party

On the day that I was born
Hermoine Granger came to visit me in the hospital
Behind a waterfall vampires sang my name
Woolworths gave out free paper nappies
Anne Frank wrote another diary about her escape
And the Queen said my name in her Jubilee address

On the day that I was born
The Titanic came up from under the sea
Cats drank lemonade not milk
School was only open for one day
Pete Waterman was kind
And all my family came to see me.

Natalie Williams (10)
St Margaret Mary's Junior School

USELESS

You're as useless . . .
As a bomb without an explosion,
As a professor without a potion,
As a gun without a flare,
As a car without a tyre.

You're as useless . . .
As a clown without a smile,
As a teacher without a class,
As a king without a crown,
As a lock without a key.

Oliver Holmes (10)
St Margaret Mary's Junior School

EVERYONE THINKS I'M MICHAEL ROWE BUT REALLY . . .

I'm an avalanche falling from a mountain.
I'm a pizza, deep in the freezer.
I'm an aeroplane up in the clouds.
I'm a riddle waiting to be told.

I'm a cactus with spiky spikes.
Wait, I'm a shark deep in the sea.
Hold on, I'm snow, freezing cold.
I'm a riddle waiting to be told.

I'm a Fanta lemon and I have just been drunk.
I'm a long lemon and lime.
I'm some very smelly socks.
I'm a riddle waiting to be told.

I'm a brand new football just been kicked.
I'm a loud blasting trombone.
I'm an alien from outer space.
I'm a riddle waiting to be told.

Michael Rowe (8)
St Margaret Mary's Junior School

Everyone Thinks I'm Laura Gregson, But Really . . .

I'm a long poem stuck on a piece of paper.
I'm a smelly sausage in the freezer.
I'm a wide blue river.
I'm a green octopus in a deep blue sea.

I'm a huge shiny football boot.
I'm a fizzy cup of Coke.
I'm a shiny bright sun in a bright sky.
I'm a green octopus in a deep blue sea.

I'm a tall, swirling planet in outer space.
I'm a guitar with broken strings.
I'm a shiny purple coat with no pockets.
I'm a green octopus in a deep blue sea.

I'm a blue square ready to be used in maths.
I'm a fast police car going to the police station.
I'm a long, tall oak tree.
I'm a green octopus in a deep blue sea.

Laura Gregson (9)
St Margaret Mary's Junior School

14th July 1992

On the day that I was born
Champagne fell in huge raindrops from lilac clouds
Britney Spears sang a song just for me
Sharks played on the bay with little fish
Footballers played football down the ward
And stars spelt my name for a million miles

On the day that I was born
Harry Potter appeared out of thin air
In a cave, cavemen sang a wild song
Next in China sold T-shirts with my photograph on
Henry VIII gave me his crown
And my mum and dad put my image on every channel in the world.

Robynn Hughes (9)
St Margaret Mary's Junior School

EVERYONE THINKS I'M HOLLIE GREGORY BUT REALLY . . .

I'm a full stop waiting for a capital.
I'm a skirt and top in an old dusty wardrobe.
I'm a broken-down car waiting to be repaired at the local garage
And I'm a dolphin in the ocean swimming around.

I'm a palm tree waving my branches all over the beach.
I'm a pizza at the back of a cold freezer.
I'm orange juice sitting in a cup in the fridge
And I'm a dolphin in the ocean swimming around.

I'm a sun shining all over Liverpool.
I'm a purple square in a dusty box.
I'm a pair of ballet shoes left behind
And I'm a dolphin in the ocean swimming around.

I'm a keyboard under an ottoman.
I'm a rocket blasting off.
I'm a beach, sandy and full of water
And I'm a dolphin in the ocean swimming around.

Hollie Gregory (8)
St Margaret Mary's Junior School

DOES IT MAKE SENSE?

Who can you brush your hair when you have no hair to brush?
How can you knock at a door if there's no door to knock at?
How can you eat a packet of sweets if there's no sweets to eat?
How can you paint a house if you have no paint to paint with?
How can you put a carpet down if there's none to put down?
How can you write with a fountain pen if you haven't got one?
How can you wear clothes if you have none to wear?
And how can you write on a piece of paper if you haven't got one?

Stephanie Needham (11)
St Margaret Mary's Junior School

WHEN I'M SIXTY-FOUR

I wonder when I'm sixty-four what I will do.

Will I go on Who Wants to be a Millionaire and win a million pounds?
Will I take my grandchildren to the park and fall asleep on the bench?
Will I go on Jerry Springer because someone has murdered my dog?
Will I have a white wedding with the man I'm truly in love with?
Will I buy a Scenic car when I don't know how to drive?
Will I buy a doll's house with all little bits in for my hamster to live in?
Or will I . . .?

Jade Clegg (9)
St Margaret Mary's Junior School

MY SECRET HOUSE

My house is in my bed,
It is made of water.
My house is painted green, gold and silver,
It is as noisy as a pub in the night.

My secret pet is a singing tarantula,
Together we sing noisy songs.
In my house I feel cool like a dolphin
Swimming in the sea.
It is as wonderful as me and my house.

Sara Walsh (7)
St Margaret Mary's Junior School

MY BROTHER

My brother is a pain,
He teases me again and again,
He puts crawlies in my shoe
And throws mud at me too.
He laughs when I fall down,
That makes me frown,
Well I love him dearly,
Well, almost nearly.

Megan Austin (9)
St Margaret Mary's Junior School

MY SECRET HOUSE

My house is in a cave where a wizard lives,
It is made of chips from the school canteen.
My house is coloured with all of the invisible spots that only I can see,
It is as cosy as my bedroom.

My secret pet is an invisible fire-breathing dragon,
Together we ride around the world on golden wings all night.
In my house I feel as mad as a lion running all day long,
It is as smashing as having my birthday every day of the week.

Josh Quinn (8)
St Margaret Mary's Junior School

THERE'S NO SUCH WORD AS CAN'T

A tiger can't fly like an eagle.
My pencil can't dance and sing like a pop star.
One rose can't have a beak like a seagull
But my nan can make the best cheese and tomato pizza on the planet.

An octopus can't play chess like a human.
Your toaster can't jump up and down on a bouncy castle when
                                        it's your birthday.
Twenty hurricanes can't run to Mars
But my friends Nicole and Josh can make the best games in the country.

A dragon can't write a story like J K Rowling.
Our beds can't go to the disco on Saturday night.
Thirty aliens can't speak human language
But I can write the best poem in the solar system.

Robert Goudie (8)
St Margaret Mary's Junior School

TWICE UPON A TIME I SAW . . .

One obedient oak, occupying,
Two technical tears, tarnishing,
Three thorny throats, thundering,
Four fabulous fractions, flattering,
Five fragile fossils, freezing,
Six scaly scorpions, scavenging,
Seven scornful seas, screaming,
Eight elderly elephants, embracing,
Nine narrow nannies, nailing,
Ten tactful targets, twisting.

Hannah Ryan (10)
St Margaret Mary's Junior School

THERE'S NO SUCH WORD AS CAN'T

A dog can't fly like Peter Pan.
My pencil can't cook like Ainsley off Ready Steady Cook.
Five lilies can't do karate like a black belt
But my cousin Tim can do any game on PlayStation 2.

An octopus can't come to my birthday party.
Fifty gusts of wind can't blow a house down
But Paul can draw like an artist.

An eagle can't lay an Easter egg.
Our TV can't have Sky on it.
Twenty-five moon rockets can't land in my bedroom
But I can be good today and every day.

For once.

Samuel Harris (9)
St Margaret Mary's Junior School

TWICE UPON A TIME I SAW . . .

One obnoxious offender, overdrawn,
Two toxic towns, training,
Three thirsty therms, thatching,
Four fetid filths, finding,
Five fast festivals, fighting,
Six scared Sabbaths, scrapping,
Seven scared sailors, selling,
Eight enormous elephants, establishing,
Nine naughty nuns, nourishing,
Ten telepathic tigers, tickling.

Jack Ehlen (9)
St Margaret Mary's Junior School

THERE'S NO SUCH THING AS CAN'T

My dog can't eat an aeroplane.
My pencil sharpener can't swim in jelly to New York.
Nine roses can't score a goal better than Robbie Fowler
But my brother Martin can fall asleep watching Match of the Day
on Saturday.

A shark can't eat the Titanic whole.
Our oven can't find the end of the rainbow.
Nineteen raindrops can't knock over the Blackpool Tower,
But my best friend Leigh can be a good runner.

An owl can't fly higher than a spaceship.
Your armchair can't open the door to the kitchen.
Thirty rockets can't fly into the sun and sunbathe
But I can score a goal better than anyone.

Andrew Lamkin (9)
St Margaret Mary's Junior School

TWICE UPON A TIME I SAW . . .

One old-fashioned overalls, oppressing,
Two tasty teams, teaching,
Three thorny theatres, thrilling,
Four frail frogs, following,
Five flimsy flies, flushing,
Six safe snails, saying,
Seven smelly saxophones, singing,
Eight enormous eagles, entering,
Nine next nannies, nattering,
Ten telepathic tests, tempting.

Catherine Kelly (9)
St Margaret Mary's Junior School

MY SECRET HOUSE

My house is at the bottom of the ocean
Behind a crashed sailing ship.
It is made of a huge ten metre shell
With seaweed for curtains.
My house is painted with sharks on the shell.
It is as cosy as sleeping in bed,
It is hidden behind a hundred metre boat.
My secret pet is a shark that can catch fish and swim
                                        at two thousand miles an hour
Together we give bad people nightmares.
When I'm in my house I feel as magical as a wizard.
My house is as wonderful as an ocean of pure gold.

Kyle Wilson (7)
St Margaret Mary's Junior School

FUN DOG TOBY

Toby is my favourite playmate
He likes to run around the garden gate.
His fur is white, eyes are black
And he likes to wear a yellow mac.
He jumped about like a crazy dog
And always tries to leap over the world's biggest log.
My friend loves to pat and stroke his chin
And Toby's face turns to a grin.
When the postman needs to call
He shouts to mum 'Keep him in the hall!'
As Toby's teeth are sharp and bright
In the past he's gave old postie a big fright.

Amy Caddock (10)
St Margaret Mary's Junior School

EAGLE

Eagle is rapid through the air
With its steaming wings.
At night and day all the time
It hunts for quiet running little things.
It's mighty beak will eat it up
And leave the bones hanging.
With its sharp eyes it looks cross-eyed,
For something to keep but not for long.
Its hanging feathers touch the ground,
And land softly.
It has its immense head,
Looking around everywhere.
He is the predator,
He who conquers always first but never last.

Peter Campbell (9)
St Margaret Mary's Junior School

TWICE UPON A TIME I SAW ...

One obese objector, omitting,
Two talkative Talmuds, teasing,
Three thirsty thrillers, thrashing,
Four fluorescent foghorns, fluttering,
Five fondest footballers, fighting,
Six savoury sausages, sizzling,
Seven savage snakes, sliding,
Eight elegant elephants, eating,
Nine naughty nettles, nibbling,
Ten tease turtles, teaching.

Laura Eaton (10)
St Margaret Mary's Junior School

THERE'S NO SUCH WORD AS CAN'T

A house can't fly to the zoo.
My pen can't run to a mouse.
Eight roses can't eat a dinosaur,
But my mum can cook for Liverpool.

A dolphin can't jump for toffee.
Our cutlery can't paint a picture.
Eighteen rainbows can't write a book,
But my friend, Alicia, can tell the best jokes ever.

An owl can't watch TV.
Your bed can't climb a tree.
Twenty-eight moons can't switch a light on,
But I can write brilliant poems.

Olivia Murphy (8)
St Margaret Mary's Junior School

TWICE UPON A TIME I SAW . . .

One obtuse onion, obstructing,
Two toxic trampolines, trickling,
Three transparent thermals, thanking,
Four flamboyant fire extinguishers, fuming,
Five furtive feathers, fancying,
Six studious squadrons, submitting,
Seven strong stretches, strickening,
Eight edible elements, examining,
Nine nuclear nostrils, nursing,
Ten triumphant turbines, trading.

Andrew Nolan (10)
St Margaret Mary's Junior School

THERE'S NO SUCH WORD AS CAN'T

A snake can't fly like Superman.
My ruler can't jump the long jump.
Twenty stars can't boogie all night,
But my mum can cook the best spaghetti bolognese.

A dog can't marry a hen.
My pencil case can't write a never-ending story.
An ant can't wrestle a dinosaur,
But my friend, Emma, can enter a dog competition and win.

An ostrich can't give birth to an elephant.
My sister can't swim a length.
Sixteen snowdrops can't win the Olympics,
But our school can win the best school in the world.

Kelsie Riley (8)
St Margaret Mary's Junior School

TWICE UPON A TIME I SAW . . .

One oblique olive, offending,
Two talkative teenagers, tickling,
Three theories throats, thrilling,
Four factious ferrules, fainting,
Five finances fires, flavouring,
Six scared salad, samples,
Seven scarlet scorpions, scrambling,
Eight earnest earthquakes, edits,
Nine nasty navels, nibbling,
Ten talented tangerines, teasing.

Wendy Jones (9)
St Margaret Mary's Junior School

THERE'S NO SUCH WORD AS CAN'T

A cat can't bark like a dog.
My rubber can't write like a pen.
Nine roses can't fly like birds,
But my mum can cook like a chef.

A fish can't climb Mount Everest in slippers.
Our kettle can't run in a marathon.
Twelve snowflakes can't make a chocolate cake,
But my friend, Daniel, can make biscuits.

A fly can't do long jumps.
Your carpet can't fly like a parrot.
Twenty-one moons can't drive a sports car,
But I can fly an aeroplane.

Andrew Burns (8)
St Margaret Mary's Junior School

TWICE UPON A TIME I SAW . . .

One objectionable orphan, opened,
Two triple tablespoons, teasing,
Three thatched thorns, thumping,
Four fine fashions, flashing,
Five fast fans, falling,
Six strong sheriffs, subjecting,
Seven silly styles, stumping,
Eight equestrian escalators, escorting,
Nine neighbours necks, kneeling,
Ten technical tapes, testing.

Michael Fillingham (9)
St Margaret Mary's Junior School

HALF AN A TO Z POEM

A   is for Aggy who wears trousers that are baggy.
B   is for Ben who is nearly ten.
C   is for Charlie who eats loads of barley.
D   is for Dilly who's always silly.
E   is for Ellie who is really smelly.
F   is for Fred who's always in bed.
G   is for Gwen who has a leaky pen.
H   is for Harry who has a mate called Larry.
I   is for Ivor who is a great diver.
J   is for Jane who's always in pain.
K   is for Kelly who watches loads of telly.
L   is for Leigh - well that's me.
M   is for Mickey, he's very tricky.

Now that is enough because this poem's too tough.

Leigh Strina (9)
St Margaret Mary's Junior School

TWICE UPON A TIME I SAW . . .

One obnoxious ogre, operating,
Two technical tattoos, tickling,
Three thirsty theatres, throbbing,
Four famous fangs, fetching,
Five fickle ferrets, flagging,
Six salty sandwiches, satisfying,
Seven sane sandals, scattering,
Eight eager eels, endangering,
Nine native nuts, networking,
Ten temporary tents, trilling.

Chloe Evason (9)
St Margaret Mary's Junior School

THERE'S NO SUCH WORD AS CAN'T

A lion can't fly and it can't read the news.
My gel pen can't walk the dog.
Nine leaves can't see food,
But my brother can play on the Game Boy for years.

A shark can't play safely.
Our bin can't skate to the car park.
Ten raindrops can't fly me to the moon,
But my best friend can draw like Monet.

An eagle can't make a birthday cake.
Your chair can't drive to the beach.
Twenty-five moons can't take me with them,
But I can play football like Michael Owen.

Michael McLoughlin (8)
St Margaret Mary's Junior School

ONCE UPON A TIME I SAW . . .

One official origin, outbreaking,
Two true trophies, talking,
Three thorough theatres, throwing,
Four flimsy flannels, flinching,
Five fantastic fossils, flying,
Six shameful spiders, shattering,
Seven shivering sharks, slaving,
Eight electric eels, eating,
Nine naughty newts, knotting,
Ten terrible tabbies, talking.

Sean Kenny (9)
St Margaret Mary's Junior School

There's No Such Word As Can't

An elephant can't write a story
My ruler can't read a book
One rose can't ride a bike
But my nan can talk forever

A whale can't jump up into the sun
Our cooker can't play tennis
Twenty rabbits can't all skip
But my friend can eat all the chocolate on Earth

A fly can't cook
Your bed can't eat
Twenty-three aliens can't all make things
But I can play the violin like Yehudi Menuhin.

Derryn Palmer (9)
St Margaret Mary's Junior School

Twice Upon A Time I Saw . . .

One obtuse ocean, occurring,
Two talkative tankers, taunting,
Three thirsty thorns, thrilling,
Four fantastic famous, fainting,
Five fierce fiancees, filtering,
Six safe swans, shouting,
Seven sensitive snakes, scratching,
Eight early eagles, eating,
Nine narrow napkins, nibbling,
Ten telepathic teachers, teasing.

Nicola Evans (10)
St Margaret Mary's Junior School

MY SECRET HOUSE

My house is on the giant's cat's whiskers,
It is made of some cat food,
That's never been washed off before.
My house is painted with the giant's egg yolk
And the roof is made of eggshells.
It is as cosy as sitting on my mum's knee
As she reads me a story.

My secret pet is a mirror
That does anything you ask,
Together we make the universe,
As we drink the drinks from Paris.
When I'm in my house,
I feel like I'm in my own world.
My house is as pleasant
As one thousand pleasant men.

Kelly Wall (7)
St Margaret Mary's Junior School

AN ADVENTURE IS . . .

An adventure is . . . getting chased by a giant frog.
An adventure is . . . saving the world with 007.
An adventure is . . . trekking Mars with Captain Spock.
An adventure is . . . having a sword fight with King Arthur.
An adventure is . . . fighting Goldfinger with the golden gun.
An adventure is . . . driving the BMW OIL.
An adventure is . . . running 5,000 miles.
An adventure is . . . finishing this poem!

Mark Johnson (8)
St Margaret Mary's Junior School

MY SECRET HOUSE

My house is in the bottom of my bed,
It is made of chocolate.
My house is coloured with the
Colours of the rainbow,
It is as private as my bedroom.

My secret pet is a dog and sings me to sleep,
Together we fly to the moon and back.
When I'm in my house,
I feel as happy as when I'm on holiday.
My house is as wonderful as
Going to school each week.

Mikey Lee Atherton (7)
St Margaret Mary's Junior School

BRIGHT

By day the sun, the moon by night,
One way or another they both give light.
A golden garden of happy children
The sun would be special to a travelling pilgrim.
The heat in the day ,
The cool of the night,
I would prefer something yellow and tight.
Bees and wasps buzzing around
Making a happy, sunny sound.
A golden child, a golden dog,
The sun takes away misty fog.

Mathew Costello (10)
St Margaret Mary's Junior School

MY SECRET HOUSE

My house is in the dark heart of the jungle,
It is made of a thousand palm trees and a million feathers.
My house is painted the dark and bright
Colours of the river Mersey,
It is as noisy and loud as two thousand tigers.

My secret pet is a dog
That can shoot arrows as high as ten flats,
Together we play baseball
At 12 o'clock on a Tuesday morning.
When I'm in my house,
I feel great, like I'm playing with tigers.
My house is as smashing
As the strawberry cake my nan makes.

Sam Pybis (8)
St Margaret Mary's Junior School

TWICE UPON A TIME I SAW . . .

One obnoxious oak, obeying,
Two technical tees, tantalising,
Three thronged theologies, thrashing,
Four ferocious fins, finding,
Five fluorescent fogs, fragmenting,
Six sealed samosas, scalding,
Seven sheltered siblings, slapping,
Eight elegant eagles, embarrassing,
Nine narrow nutritionists, nursing,
Ten tight throngs, tickling.

Hayley Simcock (10)
St Margaret Mary's Junior School

MY SECRET HOUSE

My house is at the bottom of the shed,
It is made of wood.
My house is painted with
One thousand yellow suns,
It is as cosy as cat's fur.

My secret pet is a talking dog
That can speak ten languages,
Together we play *Hang the Man*
All night long.
When I'm in my house,
I feel happy.
My house is as wonderful
As Buckingham Palace.

Joseph Haskell (8)
St Margaret Mary's Junior School

MY SECRET HOUSE

My house is a spooky cave,
It is made of dirty, old stars.
My house is painted with dirty snow,
It is as cosy as my cat.

My secret pet is a cat which
Talks to me at night,
Together we play all night.
When I'm in my house,
I feel as special as a cat.
My house is as wonderful
As Miss Cornell when she reads us a story.

Alexandra Sargeant (7)
St Margaret Mary's Junior School

Everyone Thinks I'm Laura Stowers But Really . . .

I'm a strawberry milkshake in McDonald's
I'm a beach in Spain next to some rocks
I'm a moon with a man on me
I'm a gold diamond on a beach somewhere hot
I'm a keyboard in an instrument shop
I'm a pear in a fruit store
I'm a long word that no one can say
I'm a gold diamond on the beach somewhere hot
I'm a sunny day everyone likes
I'm a word looking for a full stop
I'm a stone under the sea
I'm a gold diamond on the beach somewhere hot
I'm an aeroplane flying to Iceland
I'm a juggling ball in the circus
I'm a leaf on a green tree that's very tall
I'm a gold diamond on the beach somewhere hot.

Laura Stowers (9)
St Margaret Mary's Junior School

Here Come The Teachers

Hide behind the tables, hide behind the desks,
My dog ate all my homework, we've got a massive test.

Here come the teachers!

Eat your lunch up quick, make sure you're not too sick.
Oh no, I've missed the choir, line-up, we've got a fire.

Here come the teachers!

Victoria Collins (8)
St Margaret Mary's Junior School

USELESS

You're as useless,

As an engine without a car,
As chocolate without a bar,
As sugar without tea,
As the green of a pea.

You're as useless,

As a mouse without a tail,
As a baby without a wail,
As a man without feet,
As a shredded without wheat.

You're as useless,

As a pencil without lead,
As a room with no bed,
As a person with no bones,
As an ice cream with no cones.

You're useless.

Lee Tomes (10)
St Margaret Mary's Junior School

I DREAM . . .

I dream of a moon where blue cats fly,
Friendly ghosts dance with pretty monkeys
And a smart butterfly teaches a sad monster to sing,
Beneath the cold, dark sky.

Lucy Basnett (11)
St Margaret Mary's Junior School

There's No Such Word As Can't

A dog can't dance or speak.
My pencil can't jump high.
Eight snowdrops can't fly
But my mum can cook the best roast dinner ever.

A shark can't flap like washing on a line.
Our oven can't pour my drink out.
Eleven swans can't win the lottery,
But my best friend Andrew can tidy up like a washing machine.

A wasp can't swim the Mersey.
Your bed can't draw the curtains.
Thirty spaceships can't talk like us
But I can wash the dishes until they sparkle.

John Lea (8)
St Margaret Mary's Junior School

My Secret House

My house is in the middle of the sea.
It is built from beautiful gold with ice cream in it.
My house is painted with drawings of a rainbow.
it is as quiet as the smelly ghost.

My secret pet is a dog that talks to me when I am on my own.
Together we tell each other ghost stories at midnight.
When I'm in my house I feel as if I am being watched.
My house is as smashing as eating sweets and choc ices for a
million years.

James Dutton (7)
St Margaret Mary's Junior School

THERE'S NO SUCH WORD AS CAN'T

A tiger can't ring people up on a mobile.
My ruler can't eat food.
Five lilies can't play football
But my brother called Liam can do lots of homework.

A shark can't dance.
Your bowl can't talk to food.
Ten storms can't score a goal like Michael Owen
But my friend Jay can get us football tickets.

A bee can't drink beer.
Our sofa can't watch TV on the telly.
Nine people can't walk around Earth
But I can play the keyboard.

Sean Smith (8)
St Margaret Mary's Junior School

MY SECRET HOUSE

My house is on top of a stormy mountain,
It is built of thunder and electricity.
My house is painted yellow, white and grey.
It is as scary as a tiger shark in the blue sea.

My secret pet is a frightening, wonderful gargoyle
That protects me, night and day.
Together we have adventures all around the world
When I'm in my house I feel adventurous and jolly.
My house is as wonderful as a chocolate the size of a mountain.

Adam Walker (8)
St Margaret Mary's Junior School

THERE'S NO SUCH WORD AS CAN'T

A lion can't dance, write, talk or read.
My pen can't juggle, roar or teach.
Ten roses can't fly, flow, read, walk
But my mum can sleep for a year.

A shark can't walk on land.
Your freezer can't walk, fly, play or eat.
Twenty buses can't jump all over the place
But my friend Michelle can play football.

A volcano can't dance,
Our beds can't fly,
Twenty-three planets can't play
But I can play football with Michael Owen.

Robert Tyrrell (8)
St Margaret Mary's Junior School

MY SECRET HOUSE

My house is in a teacher's bag
It is made of sequins from a sparkly bag.
My house is painted inside as dark as the bark of tree
It is as exciting as staying up on school nights.

My secret pet is a dog that reads to me each night
Together we run around the world until we can't do it any more.
When I'm in my house I feel as happy as when I'm playing
                                          hide-and-seek.
My house is as smashing as someone's birthday with all the sweets.

Daniel Gillan (7)
St Margaret Mary's Junior School

THERE'S NO SUCH WORD AS CAN'T

A crocodile can't fly to Africa.
My gel pen can't write me a poem backwards.
Nine roses can't eat jelly to save the world
But my little brother Callum can play snooker like Williams.

A shark can't climb a mountain.
Your microwave can't swim the Atlantic.
Thirteen snowdrops can't dig a tunnel as far as Mexico
But my friend Philip can play football like David Beckham.

A dragon can't cook me breakfast in the morning.
Our beds can't wash the dishes.
Twenty-nine moon rocks can't buy me the world
But I can become a better footballer than Michael Owen.

Conor Wilkinson (8)
St Margaret Mary's Junior School

SILLY SUMS

7x9 is a date with Frankenstein.
2+6 is chocolate-flavoured Weetabix.
3-8 is the horse who had a debate.
6+3 is the sweet-tasting sea.
9-10 is a hippo stuck on Big Ben.
8x2 is a pig that's blue.
10+4 is an alien at my door.
1-7 is a cow talking about Heaven.
5x5 is a demon that's alive.
4+1 is a fire-breathing swan.

David Wright (10)
St Margaret Mary's Junior School

GIVE ME . . .

Give me the sight of the beautiful crashing sea,
Give me the sound of the wonderful squeaky violin,
Give me the touch of Michael Owen's thrilling hand,
Give me the smell of a red, shiny rose,
Give me the feeling of the spiky hedgehog,
Give me . . .

Give me the sight of the beautiful mountain tops,
Give me the sound of a computer blaring,
Give me the touch of a wonderful, smooth wall,
Give me the smell of a very cold can of Coke,
Give me the feeling of Michael Owen being my dad,
Give me everything.

Paul Pape (9)
St Margaret Mary's Junior School

SILLY SUMS

8x8 is a panda at your gate
7x4 is a multicoloured door
8+5 is a hippo in a hive
8-3 is a blue-coloured bee
9+1 is a carrot-flavoured scone
5-6 is a potato-flavoured Twix
6x4 is a cheetah that's a bore
9+4 is a policeman breaking the law
5+5 is a vampire that's alive
8+7 is a burglar going to Heaven.

Shaun Vance (10)
St Margaret Mary's Junior School

HERE COMES A UNICORN

Through the wall of thick grey fog
I saw a unicorn galloping through a golden cloak
With a lovely white mane

Through the wall of thick grey fog
I heard horse shoes and the sound of men running
And guns firing bullets

Through the wall of thick grey fog
I tasted the unicorn's breath

Through the wall of thick grey fog
I smelt smoke off the guns

Through the wall of thick grey fog
I touched the unicorn's mane and tail and its eyes.

Amy Maher (11)
St Margaret Mary's Junior School

MY SECRET HOUSE

My house is at the back of a waterfall
It is made of bamboo tied with vines.
My house is painted with fairy dust.
It is cosy as a nice, feathered duck.

My secret pet is a baby dragon that can do magic at sunset
Together we visit the queen of fairies all afternoon.
When I'm in my house I feel like a merman swimming in the sea
My house is as wonderful as David Horner.

Jack Cooper (7)
St Margaret Mary's Junior School

THROUGH THE WALL OF THICK GREY FOG

Through the wall of thick grey fog
I heard the hooves of the galloping horses
The howls of the wolves and fierce shouts of hunters

Through the wall of thick grey fog
I smelt the sweat of the hunters sitting round the fire

Through the wall of thick grey fog
I tasted the meat of the horses that the hunters were eating

Through the wall of thick grey fog
I touched the fur of the wolves that the hunters had killed
And the soft horse's tail

Through the wall of thick grey fog
I saw a burning fire with hunters sitting round it
Their horses tied up by the tent and wolves in the distance.

Joanna Malone (9)
St Margaret Mary's Junior School

MY SECRET HOUSE

My house is in the middle of a jungle.
It is made of sweets all the way from Southport.
My house is painted with all the colours from a rainbow.
It is as noisy as a firework.

My secret pet is a monkey that can speak ten languages.
Together we read poems and paint the stars in the sky.
When I'm in my house I feel as crazy as a DJ.
My house is as wonderful as David Horner.

Charlotte Fillingham (7)
St Margaret Mary's Junior School

MY SECRET HOUSE

My house is under the stairs,
It is built of feathers from a magic swan.
My house is painted rainbow colours,
It is as hidden as a cave behind a waterfall.

My secret pet is a multicoloured cat
That can speak and is as quick as lightning,
Together we travel to places
No other person has gone.
When I'm in my house,
I feel as magical as a wizard.
My house is as wonderful
As an ocean of pure gold.

Patrick Cunningham (7)
St Margaret Mary's Junior School

SILLY SUMS

7+4 is a fox behind the door.
9-5 is a horse in a beehive.
8÷3 is a talking coconut tree.
6x2 is a cow without its moo.
10-9 is a pineapple without its taste.
1x9 is a purple hen.
3+1 is a multicoloured swan.
5÷6 is a mood-flavoured Twix.
2+8 is my mate hanging off a gate.
4-7 is a dragon going up to Heaven.

Kira Neild (9)
St Margaret Mary's Junior School

25TH AUGUST 1992

On the day that I was born
The rain turned into purple and green drops
The Beatles turned into insects
A plane carried a banner saying Happy Birthday
A Jaguar painted itself blue and red
And Bugs Bunny let me take care of him for the day

On the day that I was born
The jungle leaves turned red and pink
I had a ride on a real dinosaur
An acrobat got his head bitten off by a lion
An alien blew up the Earth and people landed on Pluto
And my picture was on the front of the TV magazine.

Sarah Bracken (9)
St Margaret Mary's Junior School

SILLY SUMS

5x10 is a yellow hen
9÷8 is the Queen that's late
7+7 is a ride to Heaven
1+9 is a date with Frankenstein
3÷3 is a chocolate tree
10x6 is flu sticks
2-4 is a snake behind the door
4+2 is a biscuit made of old glue
6÷5 is an enormous ant in a beehive
8+1 is a ghost that's gone.

Christopher Johnson (10)
St Margaret Mary's Junior School

28TH JULY 1992

On the day I was born
The sun shone like a torch and spelt my name
A simple drum banged to Atlantis
Tanks fired chocolate drops
A lion turned black and white
And Triple H sang to me and my mum

On the day I was born
Money grew on apple trees
The Nazi sign turned into a smiley face
In the circus monkeys juggled with fierce frogs
The stars came out in the morning
And my dad revealed my birthday in Granada studios at 10 o'clock.

Oliver Johnson (9)
St Margaret Mary's Junior School

SILLY SUMS

3+8 is a sprout that I hate.
8-10 is my multicoloured pen.
10x2 is a strawberry-flavoured shoe.
7÷9 is a snake on a line.
9+5 is a bull in a beehive.
2-1 is a black and blue swan.
1x6 is a cinnamon-flavoured Twix.
4÷3 is a horse up a tree.
6+4 is an elephant behind the door.
5-7 is a burglar going to Heaven.

Rachel Coleman (9)
St Margaret Mary's Junior School

4/5/92

On the day that I was born
Tornadoes spelt my name out
Elvis Presley came back to life
Ambulances were painted bright pink with flowers on the door
Elephants squirted champagne
And Michael Barrymore was the lamest joke-teller on Earth

On the day that I was born
All the animals turned red with excitement
The whole of Dovecot turned into a Celtic village
Footballers came out of the dugout ballet dancing
The planets swapped places and doing so spelt my name
And every newspaper had a five page article about me
And all this happened on the day that I was born.

Rebecca Evans (9)
St Margaret Mary's Junior School

SILLY SUMS

4+4 is a rabbit that can snore.
6÷1 is a fish talking to a swan.
2+10 is a floating pen.
2÷2 is a dog eating stew.
1+9 is a lizard that can swine.
6÷8 is a talking gate.
4+7 is a cow that can go to Heaven.
6÷6 is a dragon eating Weetabix.
9+5 is a bear in a beehive.
5-3 is a counting flea.

Amy Currie (9)
St Margaret Mary's Junior School

MY SECRET HOUSE

My house is in the moon
It is built of sloppy chocolate
My house is painted the colours of the rainbow
It is as cosy as my bed

My secret pet is a dog
That speaks ten languages
Together we help to get the
Presents ready for Christmas
In my house I feel like going
On holiday to Spain
It is as fantastic as watching
Football on a Saturday.

Stephen Kelly (7)
St Margaret Mary's Junior School

SILLY SUMS

$1 \div 6$ is a rabbit scoring a hat-trick
9×7 is a cracked window going to Heaven
$4 + 9$ is a fortnight's holiday with Frankenstein
$10 - 2$ is a chocolate-flavoured shoe
2×4 is Einstein knocking at my front door
$7 \div 8$ is an ostrich who's about to dehydrate
$3 + 10$ is a dead person coming to life again
$5 - 3$ is a bear marrying a chimpanzee
$8 - 1$ is a ghost that's nearly gone
6×5 is a dinosaur that's alive.

Louise Reece (9)
St Margaret Mary's Junior School

MY SECRET HOUSE

My house is in a cave where a witch lives,
It is made of fairy cakes from the bakery.
My house is coloured with red and green stripes
And a multicoloured roof,
It is as cosy as my bed with an electric blanket.

My secret pet is a dog that can fly,
Together we fly around the world
And eat strawberry ice cream.
In my house I feel excited
As if it's my birthday,
It is as wonderful as a mountain bike
For Christmas.

Sophie Russell (8)
St Margaret Mary's Junior School

SILLY SUMS

7x6 is wine with Weetabix
9÷8 is Miss having a date
8-7 is an elephant coming down from Heaven
5+4 is a chocolate-flavoured door
1÷2 is a doctor having the flu
6x5 is a bear in a beehive
2-1 is a multicoloured swan
3x10 is a mouse called Ben
10x9 is Miss dating Frankenstein
4÷3 is a disease.

Thomas Dowd (10)
St Margaret Mary's Junior School

MY SECRET HOUSE

My house is in a deep, dark, damp forest,
It is made of chocolate.
My house is colourful, with red and yellow stripes,
It is as cosy as a leather couch.

My secret pet is a dinosaur
That reads poems with me at night,
Together we write ghost stories.
In my house I feel excited
Like I'm going on my holiday.
It is as fabba-dabba-do as watching Scooby-Dooby Doo.

Shannon Ryan (7)
St Margaret Mary's Junior School

MY SECRET HOUSE

My house is in a very hot place in the jungle,
It is built of one hundred blocks of chocolate.
My house is painted with lines and stripes,
It is as cosy as my teddy bear.

My secret pet is a fluffy cat that has a super scratch,
Together we run out of the front door
And play Snap with cat cards.
In my house I feel like putting
My red covers on my bed for my mum.
It is as beautiful as watching flowers grow.

Isaac Thompson (7)
St Margaret Mary's Junior School

9TH JANUARY 1992

On the day that I was born
It snowed strawberry ice cream
Michael Jackson became my dream
White rhinoceros came charging at me
All the parents in the world acted like babies
And stars wrote my name in silver moondust

On the day that I was born
Harry Potter put a rainbow in the sky for me
A mummy in a pyramid sang a song to me
The animals in the pet shop started to talk about me
Everyone in the Second World War said sorry to each other
And my dad went up in a rocket
And wrote my name with the smoke of the engine.

James Walsh (10)
St Margaret Mary's Junior School

MY SECRET HOUSE

My house is in the dark side of the jungle,
It is built of lovely dark chocolate.
My house is painted with gold and silver stripes
And splodges on the roof,
It is as cosy as a million feathers.

My secret pet is a fire-breathing polar bear,
Together we spread bad dreams around the world.
In my house I feel like eating a hundred pizzas,
It is as fandabidozi as a sunny hot day in Florida.

Michael Storey (8)
St Margaret Mary's Junior School

12TH JULY 1992

On the day that I was born
A rainbow appeared which had my name on
A piano played the notes from my name
A monkey jumped upon the friendly tigers
The world's most famous gymnasts taught me cartwheels
And Neptune smiled at my funny face across the man on the moon

On the day that I was born
Minnie the Minx, 'minxed' my dad
Africa's desert grew wizards to say my name
In W H Smiths across the world everyone bought paper nappies
The Romans let me rule the city
And my mum put me on TV every day
And I saw the Queen.

Melissa Marmion (9)
St Margaret Mary's Junior School

SILLY SUMS

4x7 is someone flying to Heaven
7÷6 is a coconut Twix
9+10 is a big talking hen
10x2 is someone eating glue
1+5 is a shark getting eaten alive
6-3 is an elephant living in a tree
5+1 is someone eating a swan
2+8 is a cat on a date
8-4 is a tiger with no paw
3÷9 is a date with Frankenstein.

Ernie Armstrong (9)
St Margaret Mary's Junior School

MY SECRET HOUSE

My house is in a dark, damp and scary jungle,
It is made of sloppy, horrible slime.
My house is coloured with green, blue, red
And pink stripes like a rainbow,
It is as private as my secret diary!

My secret pet is a lion who *roars* every night at midnight!
Together we hunt around the dark, damp jungle!
In my house I feel very mischievous,
It is as super-duper as listening to Pop Idol
On a Saturday night!

Eleanor Wright (7)
St Margaret Mary's Junior School

SILLY SUMS

$3 \div 7$ is a snake coming down from Heaven
7-8 is a ghost trying to suffocate
$4 \div 9$ is a teacher just like Einstein
5x6 is a pizza-flavoured brick
9+5 is a mammoth in a beehive
2-3 is a green giant flea
1x2 is a pink and yellow ewe
8-4 is a monkey kissing a wild boar
$6 \div 10$ is a toffee-flavoured pen
10-1 is a dinosaur sitting on a bomb.

Emma Murphy (10)
St Margaret Mary's Junior School

MY SECRET HOUSE

My house is where a wizard lives,
It is made of jelly from a plate.
My house is painted the colour of red polka dots,
It is as hidden as my son's teddy bear.

My secret pet is a dog who speaks seven languages,
Together we read ghost stories under the bed.
In my house I feel happier than a butterfly,
It is as wonderful as winning a golden ticket
To the chocolate factory.

Frazer Williams (8)
St Margaret Mary's Junior School

SILLY SUMS

$2 \div 4$ is a dragon behind the door.
8×9 is a nice date with Einstein.
$1 - 10$ is a blue and pink pen.
$4 + 6$ is a strawberry-flavoured Twix.
$6 + 5$ is an elephant in a beehive.
$5 - 1$ is King Kong eating a scone.
10×3 is a really big bee.
$3 \div 8$ is a hen writing the date.
4×2 is a sheep saying moo!
$7 \div 7$ is a devil going to Heaven.

Keeleigh Kelly (9)
St Margaret Mary's Junior School

MY SECRET HOUSE

My house is in a battlefield where a war is going on,
It is made of meteors from space.
My house is painted black, green and thick blue
And sloppy seaweed,
It is as noisy as everyone shouting *grace!*

My secret pet is a dog that is in the army,
Together we train at boot camp under our bed.
In my house I feel clumsy as saying I never fed the dog,
It is as wonderful as can be!

Luke Tomlinson (8)
St Margaret Mary's Junior School

SILLY SUMS

1x9 is a sum too hard for Einstein
4-3 is a pencil climbing a tree
3x1 is a swan flying to Hong Kong
5+2 is a lion at the door
8÷6 is a stick eating Weetabix
7x5 is a bear in a beehive
10+7 is a road up to Heaven
9-8 is a swan about to dehydrate
2+10 is a hen named Ben.

Stephanie Williamson (9)
St Margaret Mary's Junior School

MY SECRET HOUSE

My house is in the darkest, creepiest cave,
It is made of metal.
My house is coloured in invisible paint,
It is as cosy as a bed.

My secret pet is a lizard with fangs like vampires',
Together we give children nightmares.
In my house I feel as mad as a tiger,
It's as wonderful as watching EastEnders through the week.

Josh Monaghan (8)
St Margaret Mary's Junior School

SILLY SUMS

$7 \div 3$ is a clown marrying a bee
1×9 is a date with Frankenstein
$3 + 7$ is a monster in Heaven
$5 - 10$ is a cherry taste of pen
$8 + 2$ is an elephant in a shoe
$10 + 1$ is a moon on a date with the sun
2×8 is a concrete sausage on a plate
$6 \div 4$ is a chocolate-flavoured door
$4 - 6$ is a paper-flavoured Twix
$9 - 5$ is a ghost that's alive.

Rhian Bolton (9)
St Margaret Mary's Junior School

MY SECRET HOUSE

My house is at the end of the rainbow,
It is made from chocolate that breaks easily.
My house is coloured gold just like the sun,
It is as quiet as my sister when she is sleeping.

My secret pet is a shark that lives in the waving seas,
Together we steal chocolate at night.
In my house I feel like fighting with my sister,
It is as fantastic as my PS2.

Joseph Wilson (7)
St Margaret Mary's Junior School

SILLY SUMS

9+1 is a multicoloured swan.
3-5 is a lion that can drive.
$4\div2$ is a pig that can say moo.
6x3 is Boris the flea.
8x4 is a chocolate-flavoured floor.
$10\div6$ is a cow eating Weetabix.
1-10 is a floating pen.
2+8 is a talking gate.
5x9 is a pig drinking wine.
$7\div7$ is a cow going to Heaven.

Michael Geraghty (10)
St Margaret Mary's Junior School

MY SECRET HOUSE

My house is a labyrinth,
It is made of slime from the river Mersey.
My house is painted mouldy green
With a multicoloured roof,
It is as private as my diary.

My secret pet is a dog that says miaow,
Together we dance the night away.
In my house I feel like I'm sitting on the toilet all day long,
It is as smashing as David Horner.

Bobbi Pih (8)
St Margaret Mary's Junior School

SILLY SUMS

5x3 is an elephant in the sea
8÷1 is a non-explosive bomb
3-7 is a hippo in Heaven
7+8 is a donkey on a date
10-2 is a flea with the flu
4x9 is a very fizzy wine
9+4 is an ant at war
2x10 is a very drunken hen
6x5 is a giraffe in a beehive
1-6 is a banana Twix.

Samantha Ward (10)
St Margaret Mary's Junior School

MY SECRET HOUSE

My house is in a toy land under my bed,
It is made of Chomp bars that never melt on summer days.
My house is coloured in invisible, spotty colours,
Which only I can see,
It is as private as the Queen's palace in Liverpool.

My secret pet is a dinosaur that I teleport
From the land before time,
Together we stomp all over cities,
On the dot of midnight.
In my house I feel as mad as a door eating popcorn,
It is as wonderful as a day out at Camelot,
Which is fandabadozi!

Emma Morgan (8)
St Margaret Mary's Junior School

SILLY SUMS

10+4 is a human with a paw
4÷1 is a pink and blue swan
7x5 is a zombie that's alive
9+7 is the devil that went to Heaven
1x3 is a really big flea
2+9 is my uncle who's Frankenstein
5÷6 is a curry-flavoured Twix
3-8 is the pig that never ate
8x2 is the doctor that caught the flu
6÷10 is a multicoloured hen.

Laura Atkinson (10)
St Margaret Mary's Junior School

MY SECRET HOUSE

My house is on the darkest side of the moon,
It is built of snow from the North Pole.
My house is painted with invisible, spotty paint
Which only I can see,
It is as private as my valentine's card.

My secret pet is a goldfish
That writes poems with me at midnight,
Together we go to bed and read
Ghost stories after writing our poems.
In my house I feel like I am singing
Number one songs on Top of the Pops,
It is as marvellous as buying a ticket
To a chocolate factory.

Hannah Brodie (8)
St Margaret Mary's Junior School

SILLY SUMS

3x9 is a blind date with Frankenstein
7-10 is the worst hen
9x4 is a big lumpy bore
1x6 is a multicoloured Twix
2÷1 is Liverpool's score
6÷5 is a tree in a beehive
4x3 is a scary chimpanzee
5+8 is a panda as a mate
6x2 is a sheep who went to the loo
4x7 is an animal going to Heaven.

Thomas Mitchell (10)
St Margaret Mary's Junior School

MY SECRET HOUSE

My house in the jungle,
It is made of sharks' teeth.
My house is painted with zigzag
Stripes and a spotted roof,
It is as hidden as chocolate when I want it.

My secret pet is a dog with sharp teeth,
Zigzag stripes and it sings in the pub,
Together we play Boggle.
In my house I feel like staying
In my PJs all day,
It is as wonderful as eating chocolate all day.

Sean Rourke (8)
St Margaret Mary's Junior School

MY SECRET HOUSE

My house is in the jungle,
It is made of sweets.
My house is painted purple and pink,
It is as cosy as my bed.

My secret pet is a multicoloured dog,
Together we go to the haunted house
To see the ghosts.
In my house I feel like the Queen,
It is as wonderful as getting no snow.

Sophie Robb (7)
St Margaret Mary's Junior School

MY SECRET HOUSE

My house is deep in the jungle,
It is made of scary spiders.
My house is painted with raindrops.
It is as noisy as birds singing.

My secret pet is a frog who does magic tricks
Together we write poems.
When I'm in my house I feel happy and warm
My house is as wonderful as a great day out.

Andrea Georgiou (7)
St Margaret Mary's Junior School

MY SECRET HOUSE

My house is in the sea
It is made of sandy sand.
My house is painted rainbow colours
It is as hidden as my pocket money.

My secret pet is a whale I can go to space with him
Together we take bats from the zoo.
When I'm in my house I feel nice and woolly
My house is as wonderful as Sweetland.

Amy Brookes (7)
St Margaret Mary's Junior School

MY SECRET HOUSE

My house is in the darkest jungle,
It is made of feathers from a penguin.
My house is coloured with black and white spots,
It is as hidden as my son's teddy bear.

My secret pet is a goldfish,
Together we spread good dreams to children.
In my house I feel as happy as I am on holiday,
It is as wonderful as flying in the sky.

Jennifer Black (7)
St Margaret Mary's Junior School

MY SECRET HOUSE

My house is at the seaside,
It is made of different kinds of shells.
My house is painted all the colours of the rainbow,
It is as quiet as my mum asleep.

My secret pet is a dolphin from the Pacific Ocean,
Together we play under the water every morning.
In my house I feel happy and excited,
It is as wonderful as my mum.

Courtney Rose Wynn (7)
St Margaret Mary's Junior School

WHEN I WAS BORN

On the day that I was born
A rainbow crossed my wonderful house
All Saints sang to me
Sharks wriggled across the slippery hospital floor
All the grans in Liverpool waved their umbrellas in the air
And a shooting star sprinkled glitter on me

On the day that I was born
Mickey Mouse wriggled his big ears at me and I went really pink
I met a grizzly bear that roared my name
Asda car park was filled with sweets
Dinosaurs were cars for ants only
And my dog woofed out my name on TV for my birth.

Olivia Peremans (9)
St Margaret Mary's Junior School

MY SECRET HOUSE

My house is on a gigantic hill,
It is made of ice cream and snow.
My house is painted lilac, orange and purple,
It is as cosy as my furry bear.

My secret pet is a polar bear that can do gymnastics,
Together we scare people and laugh.
In my house I feel brill like a pop star,
It is as smashing as ice cream in the spring.

Natasha Cain (7)
St Margaret Mary's Junior School

NANNY TREE

My nan is a sweet pea
She smells of love and kisses

I love her so
I love her so

My nan's long blonde hair is no more
I still love her, that's for sure!

I love her so
I love her so

She spreads her love and care for her family
Around the world

I love her so
I love her so.

Sophie Morgan (10)
St Sebastian's RC Primary School

MY NAN

My nan's eyes are sparkly and full of joy like stars
Her cheeks are weak like the ocean waves
My nan can be happy at times, she can also be angry when annoyed
She makes my roast, I love her the most.

Richard Breen (11)
St Sebastian's RC Primary School

MY MYSTERY POEM

Money please! Money please!
The driver has to pay his fees
This engine roars
With the diesel doing its chores
These tyres run all day and night
With passengers in their sight
After our rest
Nothing else is but the best
Some of our passengers are kind at heart
While others listen to dog and other parts
With a top speed of 120mph
It's like we have got rocket power
At the end of our years, we'll be sad
For what we have done, we were glad.

Joel Richards (10)
St Sebastian's RC Primary School

MY PAP

My pap was a brilliant man,
I rubbed his baldy head up and down.
I used to sit on his lap
And watch him read all day long.
But now we miss him very much,
We want him very much,
But still we love him all the same.

Paige Kelly (10)
St Sebastian's RC Primary School

THE STORMY NIGHT

I look out of the window to see
A black sky above me
Turning and twisting
Flickering and whistling
Getting dimmer and to darken the foggy night
The sky just might
Give me a fright . . .

To hear the scary, thunderous noise
And screams from girls and boys
It strikes to climb
Up my spine
To hear a hit
Upon it
To take me to the scary pit.

Deanna Jamieson (10)
St Sebastian's RC Primary School

MY DOG

My dog is a fluffy coat made with cotton wool,
He's the best thing anyone has seen,
His name is Fozy and he looks like a sheep,
He is really cute and really small,
My dog is my *life!*

Alexandra Tavares (11)
St Sebastian's RC Primary School

MY BROTHER

My brother is small for his age,
If he had a temper he'd be full of rage.
When I have a pillow fight with him,
He starts to mess around,
I pound him to the ground.
We only mess around of course,
But when it gets personal,
We go off course.
His eyes and his shoulders
Are as big as boulders.
His feet smell like stale meat.
One week ago he did his tests
And I wished him all the best.
His hands don't look crinkly,
They look moist, he likes boring history,
But that's his choice.
When we argue, he talks like a fool,
But when I think of it, my brother is cool.

Oliver Sayonas (11)
St Sebastian's RC Primary School

NASTY NIGHT

Night floats furiously along the air,
Giving people a serious scare,
As I lie in bed to sleep,
Into my room he starts to creep.

Hidden by darkness is the moon's shine,
Then a shiver runs down my spine,
Giving off dreadful dreams,
Laughing loudly is how it seems.

Beware of the shadows,
You better watch out,
When darkness falls,
Night is about!

Kelly Dunne & Katie Mullen (11)
St Sebastian's RC Primary School

MY GRANDAD

My grandad is so good to me,
He is 76 and has wrinkles
But they are like smooth, gold sand
Raising across the contours on his face.

When he wakes up, he's a bit of a grump,
Old hump of a lump.

I still love him as a grandad
And he isn't just anyone,
He's my grandad
And special at the same time.

His smell is so beautiful,
Like daisies growing from the ground.
His fingers are knobbly and brown,
His hair is white and brown.

He sounds like an old, bitter man
But he's really nice and sweet.
His eyes are brown, brown as chocolate.

His nose is like golden, sparkly jewels
But still spotty, it's pressed down
Like a jockey being flattened by the horse.

My grandad.

Laura Corlett (11)
St Sebastian's RC Primary School

THE MYSTERY POEM

I'm in the woods all on my own,
I'm feeling scared, I was left alone,
He's sleeping,
I'm creeping,
He's awaking,
I'm quaking
And no one can see, he's going to get me . . .

I'm behind a tree, left alone,
He's rising and I'm all on my own,
He's roaring and pouring,
I'm shivering and quivering,
He's rattling and battling,
I'm hurrying and scurrying,
He's leaping,
I'm weeping
And I'm on my own . . .

Leave me alone, I shouted out,
But he didn't listen, he still ran about,
My heart is thumping,
He is jumping,
Oh no, he's got me
For his tea.

Lucy Huskisson (10)
St Sebastian's RC Primary School

MY GREAT GRAN

My great gran has soft, smooth hands
They slither past my fingers in the warmth
Her hands comb through my hair at night
I feel her nails scrape my scalp

Her hair, silky gold as the sun flows along the air,
Her bright-blue eyes glow with her hair,
But sometimes my nan can shout and cry
And I feel like a balloon floating away to the sky.

Kerrie Crawley (10)
St Sebastian's RC Primary School

THE TRAIN

Clickety click, clickety click
With the rain on the track
Clickety click, clickety click
I am on the train with my ruck sack
Tu tu, tu tu
A ghost comes to say boo . . .

The noise stops and it is silent
A killer came out and it got violent
The steam engine went for a roar
But I screamed a bit more
A high screech came from the wheel
As the paint peels off . . .

It starts clicking and then a click
And now I feel kind of sick
The lights come on
I am as white as a stoat
And those noises still go on today
And on a stormy night
You hear the train go
Clickety click, clickety click.

Lori Graham (10)
St Sebastian's RC Primary School

I LOVE MY NAN

My nan's garden is full of flowers
She potters around for hours and hours
My nan, she smells sweeter than a rose
But, never has time to stop and doze
Nan rushes around from dawn till dusk
Of a morning, she likes nothing better than a nice, warm rusk

Her favourite flowers are forget-me-nots
In Nan's shed all you can see is pots, pots, pots
When she gets a chance to have a cup of tea
It's tea and biscuits for Nan and me
I love you Nan, don't change the way you are
You certainly are the best by far.

Ruth Denson (11)
St Sebastian's RC Primary School

TERRIFYING SEA POEM

He's coming, he's coming to get me,
Creeping, creeping, creeping behind me.
I know he's there, he's coming to give me a *scare!*

He's crashing me,
He's crushing,
I don't know what to do.
He's drowning me,
He's grabbing me.

He's swirling me, he's twirling me, he's smashing me,
He's dragging me, he's pulling me into the dark depths of the sea.

Emma Carmichael (8)
St Sebastian's RC Primary School

THE TWISTING, TURNING TWISTER

I look out the window to hear a rattle
And a battle and a clattle
I'm really scared
And cannot say a word
It's coming, coming, closer and closer . . .

The sky is black, so I listen, see one glisten
Here it comes . . . but nothing, that's strange
So I jump out of bed
Bang my head
And fall . . .

I feel a soft blow
Swept off my feet, where do I go?
It turns and twists
Whistles and howls
In the morning, everything has gone . . .

Buildings in half and another soft blow
And I definitely know
A twister struck, it's in our home town
How dare it . . .

We are very upset
And can't do much
But when we get a soft blow
I definitely know
A twister struck in our home town
How dare it?

Lauren Murphy (10)
St Sebastian's RC Primary School

MY SIX SURPRISES AT CHRISTMAS

Squeak, squeak from behind the door,
I can't wait to see as I cross the floor,
A huge wicker basket, tied with a bow,
I can't guess what's inside, I just don't know,
I hold my breath as I look inside,
Whatever it is, just can't hide,
Fluffy and soft, it's full of fur,
At last I know what's hiding in there,
Six pairs of eyes, staring at me,
They all scramble around trying to see,
Six little puppies, my dream come true,
Just what I wanted, thank you.

Adeleah Dummett (10)
St Sebastian's RC Primary School

MY NAN

My nan's fresh and smells of tea,
My nan lives very close to me, around the corner and down the bend,
There I spot her with her friend,
Shining like the sun, she rises in the morning sky

And when night comes she comes down,
On Sunday she cooks my roast and she always gives me the most,
I go to her house on Sunday morning,
On Sunday morning I hear her snoring,
Her hair is as blonde as the sun and when I say goodbye,
I see tears coming down her eye.

Louise Rowe (10)
St Sebastian's RC Primary School

MY SPECIAL SOMEONE

My special someone spoils me
Her arms cover me
Her eyes stare at me
My special someone endlessly loves me
She's never cross
She's never sad
My special someone twinkles like bright stars
I especially like it when she spends time with only me
My special someone isn't very tall
In fact she's incredibly small
Whether she is big or whether she is small
I love her all the same
I don't care what she looks like
She's mine, I don't want to share
My special someone . . .

Siân Griffiths (10)
St Sebastian's RC Primary School

MY NAN

My nan's fingers are branches
rubbing up and down my face.

Her cheeks are suitcases
getting carried but then getting dropped.

Her hair is as bright as
a summer's sun.

My nan's eyes are shining sapphires.

Thomas Saunders (11)
St Sebastian's RC Primary School

MY SPECIAL NAN!

My nan's eyes are blue, sparkling waves staring at me,
Wondering who I am,
Her hands are as smooth as my silky pyjamas,
Her flaming red hair which is now as white as clouds.

My nan is not very steady on her feet,
When she walks she stumbles,
When she talks she mumbles
And when she's hungry her tummy rumbles,
When I look at her face it's as pale as clear water.

My nan is really beautiful,
I love her so very much,
I'll always be there for her.

Ainsley Hengler (10)
St Sebastian's RC Primary School

MY GRANDAD

My grandad dressed so smartly,
I sometimes wonder if he's going to a party.

My grandad always has his hair gelled back,
Did I tell you it is jet-black?

His eyes are as blue as blue can be,
Like the waves crashing in the sea.

He is a giant, a giant to me,
But if you met him, he wouldn't be.

Elena Boulter (10)
St Sebastian's RC Primary School

MY GRANDAD

My grandad's nose is
Fat and lumpy
Small and shabby
The end of it pressed
Like a button shiny and soft
It glows like a street lamp
Shining till it blows

My Nan

My nan is very small
And I love her to bits
I go to hers once a week
And when I go for a hug
She pats my cheek
My nan, I love her
With all my heart.

John Cummins (11)
St Sebastian's RC Primary School

MY NAN

My nan's eyes shine like pearls
And never seem to blink.
Her hair is a cloud resting
Into its dreamy sleep.
She always seems to smile,
When I'm feeling sad.
When I am with my nan,
I can never feel bad.

Matthew Elliott (11)
St Sebastian's RC Primary School

MY MUM'S BOYFRIEND

My mum's boyfriend smells of cheese
And has got green eyes like split peas
His face is round and very thin
His stomach is like a flat bin

Sometimes he's really nice
And sometimes he likes to eat cold rice
We're not allowed to sit in his chair
Because he's got a bad temper, *so there!*

He used to be a pancake chef
And half the time he thinks I am deaf
But my sister, Stephanie does approve
That he is a cool dude.

Channel Thomas (11)
St Sebastian's RC Primary School

MY MYSTERY SOMETHING

My mystery something moves a lot,
It moves around like a big, gold pot.
It moves around the world all day,
Trying to find all its prey.

All its movement makes me hot,
All its lines are orange and yellow
And it moves like a big fellow.
When I look at it moving round and round,
It makes me go dizzy, so I fall on the ground.

Melissa Ryan (10)
St Sebastian's RC Primary School

MY GRANDAD

My grandad is quite plump
He's got reflexes like a cat
His moustache is a prickly thorn bush
And he's mostly in a big mad rush
He wakes up at 6am and goes to bed at 12
No wonder his hair has all fallen out
And you wouldn't want to hear him shout
His eyes are shiny crystals glistening in the sun
Every day it's work, work, work until his jobs are done
Except for Sundays when he has some fun
When it comes to arguing, he's a big gun
And never stops fighting until he's finally won
His hands are like shovels, they can pick up anything
They're just like his heart, *big, warm and loving.*

Mark Brooks (11)
St Sebastian's RC Primary School

MY SPECIAL NAN!

My nan is a feathered pillow,
Her hair is as white as white.
She's as loving as a teddy bear,
She's as snug as a rug.
Her hands so soft and warm,
They are called *working* hands.
On the road she goes getting all her clothes,
I love my nan so very much,
I think she's just a soft touch.

Melissa Kelley Taylor (10)
St Sebastian's RC Primary School

SWIFTLY SPLASHING SEA

He's creeping up to me,
He's twirling me,
He's swirling me,
He's calmly creeping up behind me,
He's coming closer to me,
Oh no!

He's crashing me,
He's smashing me,
He's getting very close to me,
Oh no!

He's drowning me,
He's drowning me,
He's pulling me into the very deep sea,
Oh no!

I know he's there, he's giving me the *scare*.
Oh no! Oh no!

Rachel Johnston (7)
St Sebastian's RC Primary School

MY MUM

My mum is a lovely sunflower,
Her skin is as smooth as a petal,
She's joyful, happy, gentle and kind,
She's my mum and she's all mine.
My mum is so sweet, will buy me a treat,
She takes care of me, day and night,
That's my mum, she's so nice.

Daniel Latham (10)
St Sebastian's RC Primary School

THE HURRICANE

Midday strikes and I'm all alone
My hair's all over the place, so I really need a comb

Whistling and histling
Hustling and bustling
Around and around . . .

I'm waiting with a foolish grin
To move you in the sky

Winding and turning
Blowing and curling

And it never stopped whirling
Each day.

Natalie Murray (10)
St Sebastian's RC Primary School

MY GRANDMA

My grandma is like a gorgeous flower,
Her hair is shiny as a colourful rainbow,
When she smiles the room lights up,
Her eyes sparkle like diamonds,
My nan's cheeks are like red roses,
When I sit on her lap, I feel all warm inside,
I love my grandma so much.

Anthony Edwards (11)
St Sebastian's RC Primary School

My Nan

My nan smells of beautiful, fresh red roses,
Her eyes are as blue as sparkly waves.

Her skin is soft but with bumped veins like bumpy, white,
                                        pale mountains,
Her sneeze is so quiet as a mouse.

Her hair is short and white and straight,
The way she moves is so silent and she enjoys some fun.

She's taller, bigger than my mum,
When I look up at her she's like a giraffe.

Her smile is like an upside-down rainbow,
She can hear things from miles away.

Rachel Taylor (11)
St Sebastian's RC Primary School

Nan

My nan is the most beautiful girl,
Her eyes are as shiny as a pretty, pink pearl.

Although she has wrinkles which are like creased pants,
It looks like people have been having a dance.

She smells like succulent strawberries with a tint of creamy coconuts,
Sometimes I wish I could eat her all up.

My nan is a loving person,
She is very special to me.

Katie Mullen (11)
St Sebastian's RC Primary School

MYSTERY POEM

My special something moves a lot
I swing and spring
And dance and sing
I hold on tight
From a very high height
I have long arms
To swing along
As you know I sometimes pong
I eat bananas all day long
I climb up trees
And feel a breeze
I hang with friends all day long
Which makes our muscles very strong.

Alexandra Clark (10)
St Sebastian's RC Primary School

MY MYSTERY POEM

Splish, splash, here I come
Coming to put you in my tum
I am here every day and night
Coming to eat what's in my sight
Splish, splash, here I come
Got to save a bit for my mum
Come, come, come with me
I've a treat for you to see
Splish, splash, here I come
I hope you taste very yum
I only attack you from behind
It's a very big fright and very unkind.

Sean Ainscough (10)
St Sebastian's RC Primary School

THE MYSTERY POEM

Swish, swash, swish, swash
Down in the deep sea
Where the sea animals come to play
Where the sea animals fight their prey
Swish, swash, swish, swash

Splish, splash, splish, splash
Watch out kiddies, here I come
'Here I come to put you in my tum'
Says the shark that weighs a ton
Splish, splash, splish, splash

Smash, bash, smash, bash
Gold scales sparkle in the sea
And the great white shark was looking at me
But my mum shouted me home to have my tea
Smash, bash, smash, bash.

Gina Tyson (9)
St Sebastian's RC Primary School

THE WAVES BASHING

The waves are coming at me,
He's bashing, smashing, twirling, swirling at me,
He's powerfully coming at me,
He's bashing me badly,
He's dragging me,
He's pulling me madly,
He's crashing and bashing me.

Sean Till (7)
St Sebastian's RC Primary School